Restorative Resistance in Higher Education

Restorative Resistance in Higher Education

Leading in an Era of Racial Awakening and Reckoning

Richard J. Reddick

HARVARD EDUCATION PRESS
CAMBRIDGE, MA

Paperback ISBN 978-1-68253-837-1

Library of Congress Cataloging-in-Publication Data is on file.

Published by Harvard Education Press,
an imprint of the Harvard Education Publishing Group

Harvard Education Press
8 Story Street
Cambridge, MA 02138

Cover Design: Endpaper Studio
The typefaces in this book are Joanna Nova and Joanna Sans Nova

This book is dedicated to the memory of my mentors, friends, and teachers who dedicated their lives and scholarly pursuits toward a more equitable and just society: Charles Vert Willie, Thomas Francis Hehir, Patricia A. Somers, and James A. Wilson, Jr.

Contents

Foreword

I RECENTLY READ a story entitled "Texas Legislators Introduce Bill Banning Diversity, Equity and Inclusion Programs At Public Universities."[1] If passed, this bill would prohibit the funding, promotion, sponsorship, or support of "any office of diversity, equity, and inclusion" or any office that operates under another name but which supports the goals of diversity, equity, and inclusion. The proposal of a bill such as this did not surprise me. Still, as a person who has spent the last twenty-seven years of her life in the good fight for diversity, equity, and inclusion in our beloved higher education system, it disappointed me.

The quest to make all of America's campuses welcoming and inclusive for all continues. Progress and change are never easy—but they ARE necessary and slow. This is heart work. Because of my own journey—I refuse to be knocked off course. While this headline does not surprise me, it is jarring to me as a staunch believer that education is a great equalizer. While this headline is discouraging, I remain encouraged. While this headline is wearisome, I feel "no ways tired."[2] I still have hope. Why? Because I had also just finished reading Dr. Richard Reddick's book *Restorative Resistance in Higher Education: Leading in an Era of Racial Awakening and Reckoning*. Rich has charted the journey and created the map on how we can "do" this heart work of advancing equity for all on our campuses.

I had a noncircuitous path to the presidency, beginning with a successful fifteen-year corporate career as an engineer before transitioning into higher education. I was often the only female and, most often, the only Black female in the room. This heightened my sensitivity to the blatant absence of diversity, equity, and inclusion. I was othered and rarely felt welcomed. I had to be three times better just to be measured on par with my White male counterparts. Dr. Reddick discusses this behavior of John(etta) Henryism in this book. I decided to follow my passion for education. I changed careers and took a tenure-track faculty position teaching information technology and advising people on various career paths. This became my form of activism, building upon my belief that education is the great equalizer, as evidenced in my life as a first-generation college student. Over the next twenty-seven years, I eventually transitioned to senior administration and became deeply engaged in community activism (what Dr. Reddick refers to in the book as cultural taxation). I have been fortunate for my personal and professional passions to intersect. I have dedicated my professional career to dismantling barriers to student success—with a particular focus on students of color.

I met Rich shortly after arriving in Austin to serve as the first female president of Huston-Tillotson University—Austin's oldest institution of higher learning and only HBCU. Our first meeting was when he brought University of Texas at Austin students from his History of Higher Education course to my campus for dialogue and exchange with our students and faculty. His passion for students and their success was evident. These interactions met the mission of showing students that they are more alike than different and magnified the beauty in the sameness and diversity of our two campuses.

Our connection strengthened in 2016 when Rich agreed to lead the Education Subcommittee of the mayor of Austin's Task Force on Institutional Racism and Systemic Inequities. As cochair of the task force, I welcomed his scholarship, leadership, wisdom, depth of experience, and passion. Most importantly, our work benefited from his courage to speak the truth, stop the rehashing, and move to action. Building anti-racist institutions in all pillars of our society is everyone's responsibility. People of color do not need to be saved. They need support, resources, and equitable opportunities. While we are all equal under the eyes of the law, equity assures greater fairness of treatment and outcomes for those historically and traditionally pushed to the margins. The task force's mission was met by producing a report of over 200 recommendations to dismantle systemic barriers in finance, health, education, criminal justice, and housing in Austin. Many of the recommendations from the education subcommittee were enforced and led to sustainable, positive change that is still evolving today. Rich was an integral part of changing the conversation about race in Austin.

Contrary to what many believe, all higher education advances when we invest in diversifying our campuses, assure equity, equate excellence with inclusivity, and are welcoming for all. While Texas's recently proposed legislation to ban funding for DEI offices feels like cha-cha-cha (three steps forward and two steps back), the net result is one step ahead. I believe we all have a responsibility to "DO" the necessary heart work. There is no one correct answer, no panacea. Rich takes a very complex topic in this book and pours it into the reader as only an educator can. His "scholarly personal narrative" is a gift to us all. While the book gives him space to discuss his journey, it unleashes ideas and allows the reader to have their own self-reflection.

This is a book to help guide us through emotionally charged, brutal moments in the lives of our institutions. Rich writes about growing through serving as chair of a history committee over a campus controversy at his alma mater/employer and the ensuing mental exhaustion and fatigue of spirit. He introduces us to concepts such as restorative resistance, circle of critical friends, rarefied air, hidden curriculum, mentorability, oppression Olympics, critically teasing out and brilliantly laying bare, de-siloing, privilege payoff, and so much more.

In Andrew Davies's adaptation of Jane Austen's *Sense and Sensibility* is this memorable quote: "It isn't what we say or think that defines us, but what we do."[3] Our higher learning institutions "say" they believe and acknowledge that bias and inequity exist in our higher education systems. Following the murder of Mr. George Floyd, many of our colleges and universities published diversity statements "saying" they were committed to dismantling institutional racism, systemic inequities, and barriers to the success of BIPOC students, faculty, and staff. Yet, while boards, presidents, and accrediting agencies stand (or hide) behind their diversity statements, our campuses still struggle to be inclusive and welcoming. Despite mounds of research and data, there is paralysis as to what to "do" to support students and faculty on this quest for equity. In this work, our actions and what we "DO" are much more critical, sustainable, and impactful than what we say. Many of our institutions lack the sustainable commitment, political will, and courage required to invest in and actually DO the work of advancing equity by dismantling discriminatory and unjust structures. Even those institutions that have created diversity offices operate as though it is solely their job. It is not. Rich states it eloquently: "All members of the campus community have a role to play in engaging with and celebrating inclusion, rather than it being an issue to be 'managed' by specialists in the area—awarded this status by virtue of their identity."

While these are austere times for higher education, I am grateful to live in what can be a renaissance moment where there are "doers" on this quest of honoring diversity and being equitable, inclusive, and welcoming. The "doers" in this work are those with courage, commitment, and passion. Dr. Richard Reddick is a doer—teaching, learning, researching, advocating, disrupting, visioning, and trailblazing, and being a teacher, a learner, an advocate, an ally, a coconspirator, and a nondisruptive disruptor. All of that is captured in this book as he walks us through the power of mentorship, what restorative resistance is, and how to lead in this era of racial awakening and reckoning. He introduces us to how, when, where, and, most importantly, why we all must take part in leading our institutions toward equity and inclusion. All the while holding them and us accountable. Rich teaches us that persisting and resisting can coexist for sustainable progress to be made.

Distinguished professor and author bell hooks asserts that "all of us in the academy and in the culture as a whole are called to renew our minds if we are to transform educational institutions—and society—so that the way we live, teach, and work can reflect our joy in cultural diversity, our passion for justice, and our love of freedom."[4] I have spent the last more than twenty-five years of my career with that as my North Star. Albeit I recently retired from my university presidency, I continue that heart work as president and CEO of Newfields, a cultural institution at which the Indianapolis Museum of Art is located. It filled up my love tank to stay on course and keep doing the heart work.

Just like the everlasting pursuit of DEI work is fascinating, affirming, and completely necessary, so is this book at a time when higher education is at a crossroads. James Baldwin wrote, "I often wonder what I'd do if there weren't any books in the world."[5] I feel that same way—especially about books that stretch our thinking, spark discussion, generate ideas, are instructive and a bit therapeutic, and have a call to action. This book is all of those things. No matter where you are on your journey, what role you play, or your thoughts about diversity, equity, and inclusion, this is a book you read and then place in your books-that-have-elevated-my-thinking library. Reading this book was cathartic, gave me hope, reenergized me, and empowered me with new tools in my old and worn tool kit. I hope it does the same for you.

Now turn the page and continue your journey in this renaissance moment of opportunity.

Dr. Colette Pierce Burnette
Immediate Past President, Huston-Tillotson University
President & CEO, Newfields, Indianapolis

Introduction

I WRITE THIS at a time when the discussions on racial equity have become more and more contentious—if not outright irrational and nonsensical. It seems that the cornerstone principles of democracy—fostering environments in which everyone can feel supported, safe, and able to reach their fullest potential—are being scrutinized and picked apart. *Wouldn't it be easier*, it appears some are saying, *if we simply ignored all that makes us different?* Or even more pointedly, *What if everyone simply assimilated to the identity groups I belong to, or ones I'm comfortable with?* Implied in this rationale, of course, is the idea that our narrator would retain the resources, power, and social standing that comes with their identity. This book is an effort to respond to this mindset by validating and confirming that bias and inequity do exist in our institutions of higher education, and by expressing how they limit the opportunity and potential of the underrepresented in colleges and universities. I simultaneously show how historically marginalized communities resist these oppressive experiences through developmental networks like mentoring, and how leaders in higher education can work to dismantle the systemic processes that lead to the limiting of contributions from minoritized community members.

Before we engage in this discussion, it's important to clarify what we're talking about. I'm reminded of biologist Julian Huxley's words, which were also a favorite quote of my late mentor, sociologist Charles V. Willie: "Ideas are too heavy to carry around in one's mind unless they are rolled on wheels of theory."[1] Let's start by theorizing what I mean by the key concepts included in the following pages.

THEORIZING DIVERSITY, INCLUSION, AND BELONGING

There's a famous quote by activist Vernā Myers: "Diversity is being invited to the party. Inclusion is being asked to dance."[2] Probably everyone who works in the diversity, equity, and inclusion (DEI, or sometimes EDI) and belonging space has used it or some derivation of it. I would augment this a little: *diversity*, to me, is recognizing and inviting people from different identities to the party. It takes some effort and intentionality to make this happen—we might ensure that the party hosts represent different communities and social circles, as well as using paper invites for those who don't check email, and maybe making some phone calls to invite friends who might never have been invited before. What's important here, though, is that diversity just creates a state of different-identity people at the party. We might see people gravitating to the group they came with—important, but perhaps not meeting and mingling with people they don't know. Some people might be present at the party but immediately feel that they don't know anyone there.

How we address these feelings, then, is *inclusion*. We might create a shared playlist to make sure that our friends' favorite songs are played at the party, and we might have a wide variety of food and drink that can be consumed by all (which we can prepare for by asking what people's dietary preferences are beforehand). If someone is celebrating a special day, we want to be sure to recognize and celebrate it, and we want to make sure our party location is accessible to everyone. Perhaps most importantly, we need to recognize that this is a dynamic state. We should be adding songs and replenishing food and drink throughout the party. Equally as important, as good hosts we want our friends and guests to know that we care about them and their experiences. If we can improve the music or create more space for folks to dance, we need to make sure they know who to ask—or better yet, we need to allow space for them to work with us as hosts to make sure we're all able to enjoy the experience.

Last, as the party ends, we want to take time to reflect on the experience. Did people have a good time? Could we have been better hosts in some way? Do our friends feel comfortable and invited to tell us about their authentic experiences at the party, and are we willing to listen and make changes during the party and for our next soiree? Were we perceptive enough to notice how we might make our next party even more welcoming, inviting, and fun—including thinking about sharing the hosting role or even letting our friends who have had fewer opportunities to host take the lead? And ultimately, now that we are in a reflective space, do we feel excited and engaged for the next party? What might we need to get to that state—a good night's rest, more help from others, or even opting out of the next party until we feel restored? We should all leave the party with new stories, new understandings, new friends, and a sense of engagement.

That engagement can be defined as *belonging*. One of the preeminent researchers in this area, educational researcher Dr. Terrell Strayhorn, defines belonging as "students' perceived social support on campus, a feeling or sensation of connectedness, the experience of mattering or feeling cared about, accepted, respected, valued by, and important to the group (e.g., campus community) or others on campus (e.g., faculty, peers)."[3] We can also call it a sense that our identity is valued and who we are matters. Our party analogy attended to the ways we invited our guests, what we did to value their perspectives, and our commitment to valuing and sharing the experience. Soliciting feedback and a willingness to include different viewpoints exemplifies what educational scholar Dr. Laura Rendón terms "validation": an enabling, confirming, and supportive process.[4]

Not to belabor this analogy, but you, and people you are close to, probably have not had universally engaging and positive "parties." In cultural studies scholar Dr. Sara Ahmed's *On Being Included*, Ahmed recounts experiences as a faculty member and administrator and being the only BIPOC person in meetings—and Ahmed's dismay in hearing a leader state that race was "too difficult to deal with." A predictable pattern followed: Ahmed was charged with solving the problem and was appointed to a committee, which provided institutional cover for the lack of engagement on race and equity while simultaneously burdening Ahmed with the responsibility of being the "race person."[5] (I sense there are vigorous head nods by many of you reading this now.) Of course, this solution drained time from other work Ahmed and colleagues were presumably hired to do and was likely uncompensated and unrecognized.

What, then, happens to the Sara Ahmeds who are handed these responsibilities—as they navigate an environment where race, ethnicity, gender, sexual orientation, immigration status, ability status, and religious identity, to name a few axes of identity, are weighted against their progress? The outcomes, as I will discuss in the book, are rarely positive. It seems we must center the discussion on ensuring that all in our institutional contexts are contributing to the work of addressing racism and bias, and share in the same access to rewards, advancement, recognition, and success. This would not be "equality"—which suggests a leveling of inputs—but rather, a way to ensure that the processes and results are not limited by one's identity. Equity is what we are seeking.

DEFINING EQUITY

Researchers Drs. Uju Anya, Royel Johnson, and Liliana Garces have a robust definition of *racial* equity: "a condition in which one's educational opportunities, experiences, and outcomes are not contingent on one's race or ethnicity."[6] I concur with this definition, as the topics we broach in this book—mentoring, service workloads, and commitments to dismantling systems of oppression—are differentially experienced by those who hold marginalized racial and ethnic identities. I would additionally proffer that I am framing other axes of identity—gender, socioeconomic status, sexual orientation, immigration status, and ability status, to name some, but not all—intersectionally as we think about equity.

Indeed, the disproportional work is shouldered by many of us who work in higher education who have identities that are underrepresented in positions of power and authority. The goal is to ensure that the common goal of reimagining a world without White supremacy is equitably divided among all of us. In the words of psychologist Dr. Beverly Daniel Tatum, "To say that it is not our fault does not relieve us of responsibility, however. We may not have polluted the air, but we need to take responsibility, along with others, for cleaning it up."[7]

WHITE SUPREMACY AND RACISM

What do I mean by White supremacy? For some, the term conjures images of the Ku Klux Klan as depicted in Spike Lee's *BlacKkKlansman*—of the past, terrifying yet buffoonish.[8] But White supremacy, while inclusive of the stochastic terrorism that leads people to commit violence and havoc to incite fear among BIPOC and other minoritized populations, is also much more embedded. White supremacy is the theoretical underpinning of racism—while racism is the active expression of this theory. Anti-racism researchers Drs. Joe Feagin and Hernán Vera define racism as "a socially organized set of attitudes, ideas, and practices that deny African Americans and other people of color the dignity, opportunities, freedoms, and rewards that this nation offers White Americans."[9] White supremacy provides the social power and sanctioning to structure and systematize racism so that it moves from being simply the view or behavior of one, or some subset of the population, to a chronic, enduring status—which we call systemic racism. Feagin's definition states that systemic racism is

> perpetuated by a broad social reproduction process that generates not only recurring patterns of discrimination within institutions and by individuals but also an alienating racist relationship—on the one

> hand the racially oppressed, and on the other hand, the racial oppressors. These two groups are created by the racist system, and thus have different group interests. The former seeks to overthrow the system, while the latter seeks to maintain it.[10]

Sociologist Dr. Eduardo Bonilla-Silva further describes racism as "societal waste"—it thwarts the development and growth of human potential, and thus is harmful to BIPOC folks *as well as White people.*[11] Anti-racist practice is not something we simply do for others; we do it for ourselves, regardless of our racial and ethnic identity.

Anti-racist researcher Dr. Bob Jensen defines White supremacy as being a feature of "a society whose founding is based in an ideology that was used to justify the crimes against indigenous people and Africans that created the nation."[12] I concur with Jensen's view that the ideological root of White supremacy is in the fabric of our nation and the institutions formed at its founding. This is fairly easy to historically trace: colleges and universities are built on lands curated by Indigenous people, often without permission or partnership. Many institutions were additionally built and supported through the labor of enslaved or indentured Black people; historian Dr. Craig Steven Wilder expertly draws out this history through his excellent book, *Ebony and Ivy: Race, Slavery, and the Troubled History of America's Universities.*[13] The foundation and establishment of our field in the US and in other parts of North America are imbued with this reality.

Jensen further states:

> That ideology also has justified legal and extralegal exploitation of every non-white immigrant group, and is used to this day to rationalize the racialized disparities in the distribution of wealth and wellbeing in this society. It is a society in which white people occupy most of the top positions in powerful institutions, with similar privileges available in limited ways to non-white people who fit themselves into white society.[14]

This additional dimension to White supremacy explains the present-day impact on both White people and non-White (the term Jensen uses for BIPOC) people. Again, this is easily observed in participation rates, completion rates, and leadership in our institutions.

The point of rationalization is incredibly important, as Bonilla-Silva explains in his framing of color-blind racism. In this framing, Bonilla-Silva stakes four ways in which racism and White supremacy can be used to minimize the impact of racialized structural inequities: abstract liberalism, which is the theoretical claim of individual choice that explains aspects of how White people elect to live and attend school in predominantly White neighborhoods; naturalization, which allows White people to claim that all-White neighborhoods are natural as people from all identities prefer to live together; cultural racism, which uses stereotypes and tropes to explain the status of BIPOC in society ("these students come from cultures that don't value education"); and minimization of racism, which often grants some validity to historical racism or White supremacy but suggests that those problems are in the past.[15] I suspect everyone reading this can invoke instances of all four of these frames, daily, if not more frequently.

IN THE AIR WE BREATHE: QUOTIDIAN AND CHRONIC RACISM

Along with the systemic and structural aspects of racism and White supremacy, they are also commonplace and mundane. I like how Dr. Beverly Daniel Tatum refers to racism as smog in the air—we all breathe it in.[16] The unearned benefits afforded to White people, as writer Eula Biss suggests, result in a taken-for-grantedness that suggests that outcomes are the result of one's own efforts—and the failure of others to reach the same outcomes is, too, a result of the lack of their efforts.

> I thought "complacence" meant sitting there in your house, neither smug nor satisfied, just lost in the illusion of ownership. This is an

> illusion that depends on forgetting the redlining, block busting, racial covenants, contract buying, loan discrimination, housing projects, mass incarceration, predatory lending and deed thefts that have prevented so many black Americans from building wealth the way so many White Americans have, through homeownership.[17]

Biss further morphs her definition of White supremacy from "complacence" to "complicity," then to "debt" and ultimately, "forgotten debt"—referencing a framing that educational researcher Dr. Gloria Ladson-Billings coined in 2006 in her analysis of educational inequity as education debt.[18] Biss's reflection points to significant historical and contemporary issues that many Americans (and possibly, those across the world) are either ignorant of, misinformed about, or uneducated on. Yet the impacts of these social, economic, political, and educational policies are in the fabric of our institutions, and profoundly affect those of us who work and learn in them. This realization and active engagement is what we all need to be focused on in higher education settings.

WHO IS THIS BOOK FOR?

While I've written this book with professionals working in DEI and belonging roles at predominantly White institutions in mind, I think a broad community of people can benefit from the ideas and concepts collected here. The lines between student, staff, administrative, and faculty identity can blur significantly, particularly when discussing how equity work is distributed unequally in institutions of higher education, so those who hold these roles, intend to hold such roles, or aspire to hold these roles will find ideas of value in this book. While higher education has unique attributes and contours, people in a broad range of educational settings will find much to connect to their experiences. Early childhood spaces, K–12 schools, and nonprofits are sites of resistance, and this discussion will have applications in these contexts as well.

Last, anyone who is committing to the work of advancing equity, because of their work or even a personal interest and investment in their own growth and development, will find the contents and topics in this book valuable. Having spent significant time in community organizations, nonprofits, schools, and a wide range of postsecondary institutions, I welcome fellow travelers, regardless of how long they have been on their journey, to find footholds and navigational aids in this book.

RESTORATIVE RESISTANCE, A USER'S GUIDE

I've intended for this book be used in multiple ways. Of course, reading the book in one sitting, in a comfortable chair and with the beverage of your choice nearby, is one way of approaching the book. I suspect, however, that you don't have such expanses of time available, unless this book is your vacation read—in which case I'm immensely flattered! Therefore, I think this book works well in chapter-long chunks, and I feel you can graze in different parts that seem particularly relevant.

Chapter 1 introduces me, explains how I have come to work on issues of racial equity and inclusion in higher education, and details the concept of restorative resistance, a continual thread throughout the book. Chapter 2 is an introduction to my scholarship on developmental relationships—specifically, mentoring, and how mentoring can be deployed as a means to support and advance historically marginalized communities in higher education.

I will say that chapters 3 and 4 are something of a pair, so I encourage reading those two together. With all the chapters, though, I hope you find a community of colleagues with whom to reflect and discuss the content. With any luck the other folx will have read it as well—but it's not necessary. I did write the book with the goal of sparking discussion and dialogue, so if you have coworkers, colleagues, friends, mentors, protégés, or even particularly inquisitive pets who enjoy the exchange of ideas (however one-sided it might be), you're embodying the spirit in which the book was written.

I've described chapter 5 as an "In case of fire, break glass!" section that might be of value to folx who are personally immersed in DEI-centered campus controversies. While this chapter might help those amid a full-fledged campus emergency, I would also pair it with chapter 6, which discusses how to sustain and remain engaged in the weighty work of equity and inclusion. I also hope that you'll share how these conversations went with your community, as I'm interested in how the ideas and concepts resonate with colleagues in the field. A final plea for instructors of courses—high school, community college, summer bridge program, and first-year seminar: I really think chapters of this book could be great generators of conversation for students.

I realize that this book does not focus solely on what institutions and leaders should do to serve the goal of actuating equity—the mission that is described by the Boyer 2030 Commission: "Achieving excellence equity, and world readiness implies changes in culture—changes, large and small, often to long-standing, sometimes cherished, mindsets and practices."[19] I also want to turn our gaze to the individual and personal work we should be simultaneously engaged in. It requires humility and an understanding of the structures in which we work and learn—something higher education scholar and administrator Dr. Mamta Accapadi excellently reminds us to do: "By doing our self-work, and being honest about the power dynamic that exists across administrator/educator and student relationships, we can leverage our relationships to dismantle barriers and elevate opportunities for our students to thrive."[20]

Shall we begin?

CHAPTER ONE

Our Journeys into DEI

AS AN ACTIVE PARTICIPANT in the national conversation on diversity, equity, and inclusion (DEI) in higher education, I have observed two things: unlike many other areas in higher education, there is not one pathway to working in equity, inclusion, and belonging. Second, I often talk with students, staff, and administrators who are interested in how I came to the scholarship and practice of DEI—which recalls a statement from Malcolm Gladwell's *Outliers*: "Who we are cannot be separated from where we're from."[1]

My combination of formative experiences have provided me with a preparatory path that may resemble that of other professionals and scholars who work in this space. I also consider the unique experiences that additionally propelled me in this work, while presenting the reality that working in DEI is humbling and requires continual learning. Those of us involved in such work need spaces to discuss our journeys, such as this scholarly personal narrative (SPN), as a means for underrepresented academics to bring their voices forward, as they "have had to suppress their strong, distinct voices along with their anger, for years in the academy."[2]

I've also been told that the first chapter is supposed to provide the reader with something of a road map regarding the contents of the book! So in the following pages, I plan to share my path and journey, while reflecting on the experiences and situations that led me to this area of academic and professional inquiry. Think of this as you and me sitting with cups of coffee (iced chai for me, thanks) as we start a conversation about how we can chart restorative, sustainable work and lives in pursuit of equity and inclusion in our field of higher education.

WHAT IS THIS BOOK ABOUT?

I've been fortunate to have spent many years working in higher education and specifically researching, teaching, and writing about diversity, equity, and inclusion. I was immersing myself in DEI writings and projects before we called it DEI, simply because I found the work interesting, affirming, and completely necessary. From K–12 to university to the field of student affairs to the professoriate and to the community context, I am "doing the work" in colleagueship with many friends and allies.

The "work," however, isn't always easy. The consistent need for us to spend time and energy working toward ensuring that our working and learning environments affirm the worth of everyone can be overwhelming and draining. I have counseled many colleagues over the years on how to navigate work lives and personal lives that can be emotionally and physically taxing. This is always difficult, and the moments in our lives when racial and sociopolitical reckonings occur are also the moments when the work is most challenging, and we are in need of the most support. Ironically, these are also the times when we are called upon to commit our bodies and minds to ameliorating or rectifying social wrongs. This tension is constant and unrelenting, and many of us have paid a significant price for centering equity and inclusion in our professional and personal lives.

Despite this reality, I care deeply about the work. I find joy and validation in engaging with people with different ideas and ways of understanding the world, and at the same time, I feel I'm paying the rent for my room here on earth, as Muhammad Ali once said.[3]

Through working with others, engaging with key conceptual frameworks, and finding a purpose and meaning in diversity, equity, and inclusion projects during an infinitely complex time, I have developed a concept I call "restorative resistance." To be clear, other scholars have used this terminology—there is even a research journal with this title, but the definitions are slightly different from what I have in mind.[4] Gio Swaby's framework of restorative resistance centers "forms of resistance such as rest and joy that carry the benefit of improving mental and physical well-being," while my framing is more specific to finding reward and validation in diversity, equity, inclusion, and belonging work.[5] Dismantling structures of oppression is transgressive work, and there are constant forces working against this goal. However, finding the right pace, the right coconspirators, and the right strategy provides one with the ability to engage with these issues and retain the ability to stay in the "beautiful struggle" for equity and inclusion.[6]

I'm writing this because I worry that without committed and concerned people like you in this fight, we can't make progress. I need you, me, and everyone who cares about social justice and fairness to sustain our work so we can keep making gains and advancing on the education, policy, and social front. I hope that the ideas and concepts here can help you and the people you care about to bring about the changes we need in our institutions and in higher education. If this sounds like a good way to spend your time, I urge you to read on! I'll outline what comes next and explain the contents of the chapters.

RESTORATIVE RESISTANCE: AN OVERVIEW

Am I My Sibling's Keeper? Mentorship as the Foundation

I can't recall when I first was introduced to the term "mentoring," but I do recall being drawn to it. One of the most foundational aspects of my identity is being a dependent in a United States Air Force family. For those familiar with the lingo, I often introduce myself as an Air Force brat (which is not an insult among "brats"[7]). It means your life is marked with moves every few years, leaving behind whatever friends and familiar spaces you knew. It also means the only consistent presences in your world are your family and the jargon that goes with being associated with the military—PCS, CONUS, TDY, and so on.[8] Though I was born in Big Spring, Texas, at the age of three we were transported to England, where I have my first memories.

As one who moved around a lot and had double-digit experiences being the "new kid," I learned to quickly make friends—or avoid the bullies. Perpetual new kids seek understanding of systems, many of which are unfamiliar or obscured. You can read a handbook about the structures of the school and community you are entering, but you really need a guide. I relied on this guidance immensely, from peers and near peers, teachers, and caring adults. Simultaneously, I observed how my sister, mom, and dad found their way in the new spaces. As a result of these experiences, as we start a discussion about diversity, equity, inclusion, and belonging, I feel the most significant place to start is with mentoring.

In chapter 2, we're going to explore what mentoring is, and differentiate it from other relationships. This will allow us to explore how mentoring can lead to insight and transparency of the hidden curriculum, one of the most enduring features of higher education systems. Another aspect of mentoring is the form it will take: formal program or informal arrangement? How significant is it to have a mentor with shared identities, such as race and gender, and how might mentoring work across those lines of identity? We'll examine these questions while reflecting on what it means to be receptive and ready to be mentored, and what mentorship looks like in an era of racial reckoning and during a movement against sexual violence.[9]

Having an innate need for support via mentorship, I have been fortunate to have had several enduring relationships that prepared me for the "next thing." My mentors have only one thing in common: an investment in me as a person. Some of my mentors checked many boxes of homophily—Drs. Charles V. Willie and Gregory J. Vincent, both Black men, both members of my fraternity, Alpha Phi Alpha Fraternity, Incorporated, and both from backgrounds like mine (fellow Texans and sons of West Indian immigrants, respectively). But I have many more who are quite different: women, LGBTQ folx, and people from different racial and ethnic identities, nationalities, and even personality types. I have also had mentors who carry many of the identity markers of privilege in US higher education—whiteness, maleness, cisgender identity, upper-middle class status. They have served as translators and interpreters of the hidden curriculum, and as we forge deeper relationships, I learn that they, too, have had experiences of marginality that serve as a space of bonding.

Growing into DEI: Nomadic Origins, the Familiarity of Discomfort, and Carrying That Weight

Moving to Austin, Texas after ten years living in the United Kingdom was pivotal in my development. The late 1980s was a time of massive transformation—I was in high school, living in a racially diverse city that had some of the most rigid racial and socioeconomic segregation by neighborhood in the US.[10] Furthermore, I had arrived at the precise moment when Austin schools had finally been declared unitary, thirty-two years after the *Brown v. Board* decision.[11] My high school was located in the East Austin barrio and bused in kids from across the city—Black, White, Asian, low income, middle class, queer, immigrant, and students with disabilities.[12] We had cliques, but we had friendships that crossed these lines.[13]

Racial tension was baked into my adolescence. A racially motivated fight between two local high schools led the superintendents to create an exchange program for student leaders to visit one another's schools.[14] I hosted a peer from affluent Westlake High at my school, impoverished Johnston High. Then I visited his school—one of the most pivotal experiences of my life, as it became apparent we were living in separate worlds. Westlake had every resource in terms of facilities, resources, course offerings, and the cafeteria. I loved my school and our community, but how were we even supposed to compete in a world where some kids went to Westlake and others went to Johnston?

From that moment on, I became obsessed with the question "Why does inequity exist and persist?" and also "How do we create a more equitable world?" In college at UT Austin, I watched in horror as police officers beat Rodney King, and a little more than a year later, watched communities in Los Angeles burn as an expression of rage and pain.[15] The words and images of Anna Deavere Smith, bell hooks, Spike Lee, John Singleton, Public Enemy, Ice Cube, and Living Colour informed my intellectual development.

These sociological questions were not abstract to me; I had lived and continued to live them. I found myself in discussions with my peers and new students at UT Austin about dealing with a world where we seemed to constantly talk past one another.[16] Those who held sociopolitical power tended to see inequity as aberrations and the actions of single, bad actors, while those of us with marginalized identities saw the oppression as a system with interchangeable actors who implemented scripts that further punished and diminished people when they dared to resist.

Islands of hope emerged. I was near the front lines for the battle over affirmative action—initially calling Black students who were admitted to UT Austin in the summer of 1996 in the wake of the *Hopwood v. University of Texas* Fifth Circuit decision which banned the use of race in admissions, to analyzing the impact of the *Gratz* and *Grutter* Supreme Court cases as a graduate researcher.[17] As a faculty member at UT Austin, I had a front seat as the university was a defendant in two *Fisher v. University of Texas* cases, engaging with students, staff, alumni, and observers about why, as Cornel West observed in 1993, "race matters."[18] As I write this, yet another Supreme Court decision will likely reinterpret admissions policies. Three decades on, I'm still pursuing answers to the question. It's exciting, engaging, and yes, tiring work.

This is why chapter 3 tackles the question of who does the work and highlights the disproportionate burden of equity work on marginalized and underrepresented populations. There is research and terminology about the invisible, yet consequential labor required to move our institutions toward equity. As we discuss this, we must also consider how we ensure that our colleagues can do this important work in sustainable ways and obtain the rewards and recognition they deserve. You might see yourself in this chapter, or people you care about—and you may hold a position of leadership that empowers you to intercede and disrupt systems that add additional labor without recognition and representation.

Distributing Equity Work and Responsibilities, Equitably

Equity is often discussed in terms of outcomes but should also be framed in terms of responsibility. As an early-career scholar, I associated with my peers on projects designed to address structural barriers to advancement. A cohort of my graduate school classmates and I created a space of convening and healing called the Alumni of Color Conference at the Harvard Graduate School of Education.[19] The amount of time and commitment it took to conceptualize, launch, and sustain the conference simply became part of our (and our families') lives.

These commitments continued in my career, and the combination of supporting students who have experienced marginalization, pursuing research that intends to disrupt and reimagine structures in higher education, and serving as a bridge between institutions and the communities we are supposed to serve is sometimes overwhelming. After researching and analyzing the narratives of students, staff, and faculty taking on additional duties and labor in service of creating more inclusive campuses, it dawned on me that implicitly (and in some cases, explicitly), the majority members of the campus community were accruing time and opportunities because of the disproportional, inequitable workload placed on our most marginalized populations.

This realization underpins chapter 4, where we'll explore the flip side of cultural taxation, which I have termed the privilege payoff. We will engage with the literature and research on faculty workloads and phenomena such as social loafing, and apply a lens to how they impact marginalized faculty—women, BIPOC individuals, queer people, people with disabilities, international citizens, and other groups underrepresented in power structures at predominantly/traditionally/historically White institutions.

Tellingly, challenging the embedded assumptions that equity and inclusion work somehow belongs exclusively to underrepresented populations requires a mindset shift, and that is embracing diversity, equity, inclusion, and belonging as the responsibility and aspiration of the entire campus community. We also will frame equity work as strength, a necessary strategy when one considers how political actors have attempted (and succeeded in some instances) to weaponize the work to make campuses more inclusive as dangerous or antidemocratic. This very real threat to nascent efforts to broaden access to our institutions is chilling, and we will examine the reality of equity work in a time of "double pandemics"—COVID-19 and the chronic illness of racial injustice—when our efforts are more necessary than ever.

Emotional Entanglements with Our Complex Pasts and Present

Equity and inclusion labor often means working in spaces where complex and deeply complicated issues lurk. As a resident Texan adjacent to the American South, I can attest that many of our symbols and ephemera are mired in the legacy of the Confederacy, even down to the names of schools, teams, spirit groups, and newspapers—activities I, as a Black student with my Chicano/a, Asian, and White classmates, engaged with.[20] Even as a high schooler, I found myself enmeshed in these debates: What do we do with the troublesome aspects of our history? Do we erase, reinterpret, add—or some mixture of these options? As we live in what historian Peniel Joseph terms the "third reconstruction," those questions are becoming more relevant, more pointed, and frankly, more likely to occur at a campus near you.[21]

That certainly was the case for me in the past few years, when a campus controversy centered on the origins, performance, and impact of "The Eyes of Texas," a venerable part of the university's spirit and traditions, the school song.[22] My focus shifted from that of an alum of the university to a scholar of higher education and its requisite history and problems to a university representative charged with leading the scholarly inquiry of the song.

Chapter 5 uses the controversy over "The Eyes of Texas" as an issue that evades simple solutions and begs us to grapple with the complexities of emotion, rational thought, history, and media. While the content of the research and analysis that our committee produced is accessible elsewhere, the chapter delves into the experiences surrounding a white-hot campus conflict that resonated in the community both proximal to and distant from the institution.[23] As a case study, I will outline the issues and the evolution of a project to lay a foundation for conversation, examination, and discussion about the song (and therefore, the university, city, and state's history). Rather than giving a dispassionate review of the events, I will delve into the more challenging aspects of the work and the impact it had on my well-being and development—too often forgotten or relegated to the margins of discussions on those who participate and lead discussions around highly emotional, combustible debates. Here, some of the work around equity and campus cultures provides a framing for how others can think about similar concerns at institutions across the higher education sector.

Restorative Resistance and Sustainable Struggle: How We Live in the Crucible of DEI

From modes of mentoring, to understanding how the weight of equity and inclusion work falls on the shoulders of marginalized members of our communities, to centering the focus of equity work (or lack thereof) on those with privileged identities in the field, and finally to how higher education leaders might lead the multifaceted discussions on diversity and inclusion, we end the book by discussing restorative resistance—an approach to capacity building and community orientation that centers on self-care for diversity, equity, inclusion, and belonging scholar practitioners.

I draw on the analogy of committing to a lifestyle of fitness and wellness to express how equity-focused professionals can thrive even with the significant pressures and constant work at predominantly White institutions, supported with balance and by a community of support. Borrowing from concepts such as tempered radicalism and critical friend circles, the goal is to articulate a presence in equity work that can endure over time. At the same time, I advance the importance of concentrating on one's health first and foremost, and discuss how in some cases, for some people in the work, taking time away from the essential work of equity is radical, necessary, and the best decision one can make.

At this point, you've made it through the entire book. I expect you'll have questions, some good conversations, and hopefully, some ideas and directions about how to engage in equity work on a professional, academic, and personal level. I raise my beverage of choice to yours and humbly say, "Thank you"—and lend it to a friend to read!

MY JOURNEY INTO DEI

College Days Swiftly Pass

As I've outlined, my investment in diversity, equity, and inclusion goes back to the 1980s (when we used terms like "racial sensitivity training" to describe it), from high school to college, where as an orientation advisor I cofacilitated discussions on diversity and inclusion with hundreds of incoming students to the University of Texas at Austin. In retrospect, I think about how visionary our Office of the Dean of Students leadership was in requiring that all orientation students participate in the "diversity program" as well as our program on sexuality and decision-making. As peers facilitating discussions with fellow classmates, we saw every imaginable outcome: stunned silences, angry outbursts, emotional outpourings. Diversity and inclusion was my unofficial, undeclared major via my activities and involvement on campus.

But while my "day job" was working with professionals in the field of student affairs, I spent much of my time as a resident advisor. I was an unusual choice for an RA: introverted, choosing to live in a residence hall in my hometown (thanks to my scholarship), and one of a handful of students of color in Dobie Center. But our resident director Alan, who'd grown up in South Africa and Houston, had a plan to build a diverse staff that reflected the burgeoning diversity on campus. I immediately bonded with Marcus, a fellow student who became my best friend and accomplice on many adventures negotiating race and identity, even in our postcollege days when we were roommates. I also made friends with different identities and backgrounds than mine, and we worked together to create a supportive environment for our residents as well.

I'm proud that our friendships have endured—I have often discussed these issues with Marcus, and Scott, another RA buddy over the years, and that the authentic learning that happened in dorm hallways, cafeterias, and each other's rooms has stayed with us and impacted how we see the world, how we raise our children, and how we understand social justice. Between facilitating discussions in orientation, working in the Welcome Program for African American and Hispanic Students under the mentorship of Mrs. Brenda Burt, and serving as an RA, I was living student affairs 24/7 . . . and enjoying *most* of it. My immersion in issues of social justice has been long-standing, but at that stage of my life, it was all-consuming, and I did not know how to balance and periodically step away from the work. I know there were semesters when my grades suffered because my mind and energies were elsewhere, and I internalized a lot of the stresses in advocating for a more inclusive campus environment. Because the movement to create more hospitable climes was nascent, I'm not sure if we had messages about how to care for ourselves and permission to prioritize our own well-being, as I discuss in this book.

The Education Profession as a Space of Engagement

I was inspired to be part of a movement toward creating educational opportunities for low-income students of color, much like me. I applied for and was accepted to Teach For America and taught at E. O. Smith Educational Center in the Fifth Ward community in Houston, Texas with a cohort of passionate new educators, Shelia Williams and Matt de Ferranti. We became a loyal circle of critical friends, challenging and supporting each other to be better teachers and to engage with our students and families. As much as I was invested in working in my classroom with students for high academic achievement, I got to observe and engage with community organizations like Fifth Ward Enrichment, led by "Mr. Mac"—Ernest MacMillan, community activist, and my roommate and best friend Marcus's uncle. Here, I learned that the complex social inequities in our communities needed interventions on the individual and systemic level, as well as inside schooling systems and outside of them.

I suppose these observations and the support of community members like Mrs. Eunice Alexander, our Title I coordinator, and Mrs. Betancourt, our school custodian, inspired me to take on a new, unprecedented challenge—graduate school. I applied to one school because I had met a doctoral student who was interning in the Houston Independent School District and served on a superintendent's advisory council with me. Valencia Douglas was such an impressive presence on the committee, I had to ask her how she learned to lead and engage with such confidence. She told me that her experience at the Harvard Graduate School of Education had been transformative, and perhaps it would be a place that could serve that role for me.

Despite Valencia's urging, I thought Harvard was a dream beyond my grasp; I didn't have a sky-high GPA (largely because I leaned into campus climate work at times more than my studies). In addition, I wanted to return to my passion of working with undergraduate students. I wondered if there were teachers that focused on higher education, and so requested Harvard's viewbook (back in 1998, very few institutions had websites). Reading through its pages, Harvard's Graduate School of Education (or HGSE) did seem like a place that might fit my goals. There were teachers and administrators like Drs. Charles V. Willie, Judith Block McLaughlin, and Stacy Blake. I decided to put my hat in the ring and apply, sight unseen (unless you include a quick drive-by of Harvard's campus from the Boston side of the Charles River when I was in Boston taping the 1993 *Wheel of Fortune* College Week championship). I didn't have a backup plan because I hadn't researched other graduate schools. In my mind, I was either going to be in the intellectual hub of Cambridge, Massachusetts, or . . . I actually had not thought that through.

The Graduate School Journey, Phase One

Fortunately, that plan did work out. I convinced my girlfriend-soon-to-be-fiancée, Sherry, to move with me to Cambridge for the year. Again, it was a one-year plan. What came after, we would figure out together. After our move, we met Brooke Tippens, a fellow incoming student who lived a few buildings down. One day Brooke and I had the idea we should visit campus and get to know the buildings. As we arrived on the fourth floor of Gutman Library, we immediately saw Dr. Charles Willie in front of his mailbox. Brooke urged me to say hello and introduce myself—and I rapidly discovered our common bonds. Dr. Willie was a Texan, from Oak Cliff in Dallas. He was also a member of my fraternity, Alpha Phi Alpha. After our discussion, Dr. Willie laughed, saying, "It's a pleasure to meet a Texas scholar." It was a warm initial meeting with my first academic collaborator and lifelong mentor.

Brooke also introduced me to Frank Tuitt, who was a student at HGSE. I was soon working with him as an intern in the residence life and student programming office at the Massachusetts Institute of Technology (MIT). Frank had similar interests to mine—How do we help students of color navigate a space that could be indifferent, even hostile to their needs and concerns? We worked on programming with students, much like the work I had done as an undergraduate orientation advisor, but this time with the film *The Color of Fear*. Frank knew his way around MIT and Harvard, so

I played the role of ingenue, learning all I could from him. Tapping into my military brat sensibilities, I realized Frank was going to be a longtime mentor and advisor.

We had the benefit of working with Katie O'Dair, herself a rising student affairs star at MIT. Katie had boundless confidence in us and trusted us when we proposed ideas for programming. Katie also sought resources for us to attend professional convenings—including the National Association of Student Personnel Administrators (NASPA) conference, where one could participate in a "placement exchange" for jobs across the nation—and paid my conference fees. As I approached graduation at Harvard, I saw an ad posted on a bulletin board at the NASPA conference for a position at California Polytechnic State University, San Luis Obispo. A few interviews and weeks later, I accepted a position as a coordinator of student development at Cal Poly as a freshly minted master's graduate-level professional.

First Forays into Student Affairs

At Cal Poly, I met student affairs professionals who were eager to help me transform from the intern role to being a new professional. Soncia Reagins-Lilly, who worked with student government, was a kind and interested colleague. Little did I know we would work together as faculty members and colleagues at UT Austin a decade later. We found a social circle of Black, Latino/a, queer, and Asian professionals on campus. I became close to many, particularly my "big boss" Preston Allen, who was always available and accessible to me. I shared professional concerns that I only felt comfortable asking another Black male.

Preston invited his college buddy Dr. Jeff Milem to give a talk at Cal Poly and ensured that I had an opportunity to meet with him—which in turn led me to the work that he, Drs. Sylvia Hurtado, Eric Dey, and Patricia Gurin were embarking on at the University of Michigan. There was a developing area of social science research specifically exploring the benefits of racial diversity on college campuses . . . something I was interested in, perhaps, if I ever returned to grad school for a doctorate (which seemed very distant, considering I was still ruminating, reading, and reflecting on my master's experience). Jeff was another role model and mentor who would be important in the years ahead as president of the Association for the Study of Higher Education, an advisor for the higher education program at UT Austin that I would co-lead years later, and a faculty member in the Bravely Confronting Racism institute I currently co-lead.

Another leader I connected with was Dr. Juan Gonzalez, vice president for student affairs. Seeing a man of color as a vice president of the university conveyed to me another dimension of possibility, and that perhaps a role such as his would be in my future. Once again, years later, I would be a colleague of Juan's at UT Austin. I am not sure what stars aligned that placed me in this midsize school in Central Coast California, but to this day I find it remarkable that so many impactful mentors, role models, and guides in my development as a student affairs professional and scholar would intercede in my life in those two years.

My next role in student affairs was as an area director at Emory University in Atlanta, where I had a terrific staff. I worked with Dr. Brit Katz, who exemplified servant leadership, Melissa Trifiletti, who showed me how to navigate difficult work relationships with patience, humor, and a little steel if needed, and Sherry Ebrahimi, who radiated positivity and an ability to find joy in even the most challenging situations. Atlanta was a good place for a young couple—not too far from Texas and surrounded by Black excellence everywhere. However, the tight-knit community of Black and Brown colleagues that I'd had throughout virtually all of my educational and professional experiences was more distant. I started to notice the paucity of Black men (and women) in my student affairs space. Colleagues at nearby universities and those I would see at conferences were vital, but I now had less certainty about advancing in my field. Who were going to be the mentors to bridge the professional aspects of the work with the unwritten rules and hidden curriculum—that only senior leaders of color seemed to understand and translate?

This question coincided with a call from the HGSE Office of Admissions asking me to share my master's experience with prospective students. I shared how in a year I had found a community that intellectually challenged me, and how I had grown under the tutelage of Dr. Willie. At the mention of his name, the other panelists chimed in with Dr. Willie stories—his care, his concern, and the rigor of his courses. It was astonishing to see how Dr. Willie had done this for so many others, for many years.

Soon after, Frank Tuitt, now a few years into his doctoral studies, suggested I come to visit HGSE on student of color recruitment weekend to touch base with Dr. Willie and meet some of Frank's classmates. We reconnected with old friends and met a new group of students. I met Sonja, Heather, Antonio, Louie, and Lionel, and another student we hadn't met, Dorinda, kindly allowed us to stay in her apartment while she was out of town. It was the same camaraderie I had experienced as a master's student, but more intense—these folks were around each other for years, not just the one we experienced as EdM students. I also heard them discussing recruiting students of color and faculty of color, and looking to hire a staff member to care for students of color in the school. I found myself drawn to the strategizing and discussion. I'd missed all of it.

We arranged to meet with Dr. Willie over the weekend in his office. After our pleasantries, Dr. Willie brought up the final paper I'd written for his Minority and Majority Families course. I had asked to write a case study of same-sex families, and Dr. Willie agreed. In interviews, gay and lesbian families shared their challenges—as there was no legalized same-sex marriage in Massachusetts at the time, they had expended thousands of dollars to ensure that each parent could pick up their child from school, and other aspects of family life that straight married couples took for granted. It struck me as incredibly unfair that they were only able to approach equity by virtue of paying substantial amounts for legal protections simply granted to married couples—What about the lesbian and gay couples who didn't have access to those resources? When I got the paper back from Dr. Willie, he declared it "worthy of publication in a journal," and assigned it an "A." This paper was still on Dr. Willie's mind three years on, and he mentioned that he was looking to write a new edition of *A New Look at Black Families*.

"Would you be interested in writing the next edition with me?" he asked.

On our way back to Atlanta, I asked Sherry if she heard Dr. Willie ask me to write with him—she had. I reached out to Frank and asked him how this might work. "You need to apply for the doctoral program, discussing the book and your interest in mentoring," he replied. I immediately went about scheduling a GRE test and started on the statement summarizing my interest in writing about minority and majority families, and the need for theories about mentoring for professionals of color in student affairs. I submitted everything and immediately thought that it was too rushed and that I would probably need to think about applying again the following year.

In March 2001 I received a phone call from my organizational theory professor, Dr. Stacy Blake-Beard. She was excited to tell me that I'd been admitted to the doctoral program, and we would be working together. I couldn't believe my luck—working on a project with Dr. Willie and being advised by Dr. Blake-Beard. A year after moving to Atlanta, we were once again moving back to Cambridge. We left Atlanta just as we were getting to know it and Emory, but we were looking forward to the second chapter of the HGSE experience.

Doctoral Dilemmas: Practice, Research, or the Academy?

Dr. Willie—or Chuck as I would gradually get to know him as—was an applied sociologist, bringing his research from the academic realm directly to practice, in venues as varied as Boston Public Schools, the Carter administration, and the Episcopal Church. We worked on two books: one continuing his groundbreaking research on the strengths of Black families, and the second a nascent research project that became a defense of historically Black colleges and universities (HBCUs). Frank Tuitt introduced me to Carolyn Howard and Dr. Dean Whitla, principal investigator of the Harvard National Campus Diversity Project. This project had us investigating and researching best practices supporting students, faculty, and staff in their pursuit of diversity on campus as we visited over thirty universities and met with various members of the community—we originally intended to visit over one hundred, but the tragic events of September 11, 2001, led to a number of campuses opting out of our study. Understandably, they had to focus on supporting their community members during a difficult time. We were grateful for the schools who agreed to remain in the study.

I had entered my doctoral program with the goal of working in the student affairs field; I had never thought about becoming an academic. My own dissertation research on the mentoring practices of Black and White faculty mentors of Black undergraduate students, however, did have me thinking about what one of my participants termed "the life of the mind." As a first-generation collegian, I didn't really know that one could be a professor doing the work I was interested in engaging with. But I had prodding, from Dr. Willie, Dr. Whitla, and mentors like Drs. Susan Moore Johnson, Vivian Louie, Richard Chait, Tom Hehir, and my advisor Dr. Bridget Terry Long. Slowly, as I simultaneously watched my colleagues like Frank Tuitt enter the professoriat, I started to believe that I could teach and research, too.

A Sort of Homecoming: Research, Teaching, and Living in Austin

I had no idea how to conduct a faculty position search, as many doctoral students in my circle had done. However, in 2007, the educational leadership departments at UT San Antonio (UTSA) and UT Austin both had searches for higher education scholars, and those were the only two searches I entered. I had incredibly rewarding visits to both institutions and met supportive colleagues and students. Yet the opportunity to return to my alma mater as a faculty member was irresistible, and I joined the faculty at UT Austin in August with another higher ed scholar, Victor

Sáenz, who had also attended UT Austin during the early 1990s. We called our experience an "accidental cluster hire": in the literature, cluster hiring means that departments hire more than one underrepresented faculty member so that the new professors have a community of support in their new positions.[24] I credit our departmental colleagues and Dr. Greg Vincent, then vice provost for diversity and later the inaugural vice president of diversity and community engagement at UT Austin, for the advocacy to bring us both to our alma mater.

As an early-career scholar, I found myself somewhat overwhelmed by the three "legs of the stool" that comprise faculty life—research, teaching, and service. I was new to the first leg but found validation and familiarity in the latter two. Serving as a faculty member in my hometown provided many opportunities to partner with schools and community organizations. I returned to the campuses of schools I had attended in East Austin and South Austin to inspire youth to pursue their college dreams, and I helped found Montessori For All, the city's first public Montessori school in East Austin. I loved teaching master's and PhD students, and even found a way to teach in the Plan II Honors Program, as director Dr. Michael Stoff invited me to participate in the Perspectives course with some of the university's most distinguished faculty. I was fortunate to be recognized with several teaching awards and taught a signature course for first-year students on higher education, Alma Matters. While I had found a foothold in teaching and service, mentors external to UT Austin reminded me I wouldn't earn tenure, even with a strong teaching and service record, without a rigorous and focused line of research.

I found the journal submission process intimidating. I knew I wasn't supposed to take the feedback personally, but reviewers who questioned the significance of studying mentoring across race or the sampling methods and analysis I employed made me question if I in fact knew what I was doing. Impostor syndrome kicked in, and I found myself somewhat adrift, unsure if I would have the requisite research to reach tenure.[25] My mentors, however, had a plan.

Intercessing Mentors: A Scholarly Lifeline

Dr. Willie, my now three-time coauthor as we wrote yet another edition of our book on Black families while I was on the tenure track, reached out to tell me I should connect with his protégé Dr. Richard Hope at the Woodrow Wilson National Fellowship Foundation. As I was about to start my third year on the tenure track, Dr. Hope told Dr. Willie that I should be in touch with him again. Dr. Hope encouraged me to apply for the Foundation's Career Enhancement Fellowship, which would provide a year of funding to work on research in preparation for promotion and tenure. My duties as a program coordinator and my teaching responsibilities had led to a somewhat lagging research record—having a year to focus expressly on getting articles out, revising manuscripts, and finishing projects would prepare me for tenure.

I received word on Valentine's Day that I would be a 2010–11 fellow. Soon after, our second pregnancy unexpectedly became "high risk," and in April, our second child Katherine arrived nine weeks premature. We spent virtually every day for the next three months in the neonatal intensive care unit at St. David's North in Austin, where the nurses cared for our tiny daughter until she was able to come home. I remember virtually nothing from this time except the kindness of my students, who were mostly community college leaders that understood how life circumstances often intersected with their students' academic pursuits—turns out this was true for professors, too. Katherine was healthy and at home by the summer, and while I did not know *exactly* how to use a faculty leave, I created enough space to work on those articles.

This momentum led to acceptances that were previously so fleeting. In particular, the academic partnership and friendship I had established with Dr. Kimberly Griffin going back to our graduate school days developed into a publication in the *American Educational Research Journal*, one of the most esteemed and competitive journals in the field of education, an article that several scholars have used as a model, with over 200 citations.[26] My Career Enhancement Fellowship year was one of incredible productivity and reprioritizing family—precisely what the fellowship was designed for. I was tenured and promoted to associate professor in 2014, which was something I never expected would happen, and rarefied air for a first-generation collegian.

I now sensed that I could pause a bit, but my mentors collaborated to push me onward. I think of the champions I had in Drs. Kristen Renn and Marybeth Gasman, who took interest in me as a scholar and provided opportunities to advance my scholarship and position my research in visible spaces, and Dr. Mark Gooden, who had a clear-eyed view of the academy and helped me think two steps ahead of where I was. Another was Dr. Bob Jensen, who I'd long admired, who had taken an interest in my career.

Midcareer Meditations: What's Next?

During one of our regular Thai lunches where we would discuss the state of our research, the university, and world affairs, I was telling Bob Jensen of my ambivalence about the grind to reach full professor: now that I had tenure, I wasn't convinced it was worth the time and sacrifice. Bob leaned in closely and said, "I don't think this is really a choice for you. Your commitments, the things you value, the changes you're committed to in the academy . . . you *need* to be a full professor." Bob's own commitments to radical feminism, anti-racism, and systemic change doubtless inspired this insight, and I silently considered his words. This advice resonated with me, and I strategized with mentors like Drs. Mark Gooden and Rich Milner on publications, serving on editorial boards, and other ways to demonstrate leadership in the field.

As I was establishing a foothold in the academic world, an old mentor and friend reappeared. Dr. Joe Zolner, who had hired me as a first-year doctoral student to facilitate discussions with higher education professionals in the Harvard Programs in Professional Education, asked if I'd be interested in leading a session on diversity, equity, and inclusion for the Management and Leadership in Education (MLE) institute. Impostor syndrome set in: There were so many people doing this work, more experienced, more cited, surely someone else would be better? Joe was prepared for this—he knew that my publications and research as well as my style of teaching would contribute to the institute. I recall telling the group what a full circle moment it was for me, lecturing in the same classroom where I took most of my first-year doctoral classes. For a first gen kid like me, it didn't get any more nerve-racking . . . yet validating, than this.

Leading professional education sessions at Harvard built my confidence. I realized that the curiosity, engagement, enthusiasm, and humility that was inherently part of facilitating professional development courses was something I both enjoyed and derived a great deal of inspiration from. I got to work alongside old friends and heroes—college presidents Drs. Beverly Daniel Tatum and Freeman Hrabowski, and my HBCU research collaborator Dr. Jim Honan. After reconnecting after a session, Jim asked me to not only teach in the Institute for Educational Management (IEM), but also consider serving as IEM faculty cochair with him: a more permanent role helping to shape the institute that developed higher educators for almost fifty years. The opportunity was too great to pass up, even if I didn't quite know how it would work from two thousand miles away. I realized I could also build bridges back to Harvard for my graduate students, presenting at the Alumni of Color Conference with them.

This career prospect coincided with a change back at the UT College of Education—a new dean search. I was thrilled that our college would be led by Dr. Charles Martinez—a former chief diversity officer at the University of Oregon. Charles immediately announced that the college would have a new associate dean focused on diversity and equity issues, something our ad hoc college committee had advocated for. Our collective work on the Council for Racial and Ethnic Equity and Diversity (CREED) involved advocating for similar roles for every college and school at the university. I was interested in this role; it seemed to match what I'd been doing at the college, university, community, and national level for some time. I thought of the associate deanship as a container for my various community and equity commitments—the opportunity to do them with an eye to the future of the College of Education was an exciting new dimension of the work.

Associating with Administration

At the end of spring 2019, after a rigorous interview process, I was named the first associate dean for equity, community engagement, and outreach for the UT College of Education. We hit the ground running with a new process for increasing diversity in our search processes, implicit bias training for our search committees, and creating an inclusive, equity-centered template for all our job postings.

I also became part of a national network of diversity officers in colleges of education, led by Drs. Anneliese Singh at Georgia and Michelle Bryan at South Carolina. Many of us were in inaugural roles and had diffuse and diverse responsibilities. I began to appreciate the structural aspects of my job focus. The space I most frequently worked in had to do with ensuring that our pools were diverse and assisting in our retention offers for faculty; some of my colleagues didn't have a clear focus in their role. A similar group came together at UT with similar reflections—we all had "diversity" and/or "equity" in our titles, but our jobs differed. Some were more student facing, others deep in the machinery of college operations, and yet others still in flux.

As I was learning the rhythm of college leadership, teaching, and research, the pandemic forced us all into a period of triage and rapid learning about online teaching and engagement. Months later, we all witnessed the nine-minute murder of George Floyd. My job as associate dean, and indeed as a scholar of race in higher education and society became more intense, more consuming, and more taxing. My own personal well-being suffered, as the anxiety of raising Black children in a sociopolitical reality that places less value on their lives compared to their White peers sank in. I remember a basketball game with my thirteen-year-old son Karl when I asked him how he felt about the George Floyd murder, and my slow realization that through the deaths of Philando Castile, Breonna Taylor,

Sandra Bland, and others, he had a "vocabulary" about the regularity of Black people being killed in extrajudicial ways. How much of his innocence and childhood had been occupied by weighty issues such as police killings of young Black people?

All of us doing work in the diversity, equity, inclusion, and belonging space have had an unprecedented expansion of our roles since 2020. Supporting communities who felt excluded in our institutional spaces has brought additional challenges and opportunities. As people who work as helpers, we may be neglecting our own health and well-being. Dr. Robbin Chapman at Harvard's Kennedy School of Government and I have cochaired a professional education institute entitled Bravely Confronting Racism, directly engaging with institutional leaders taking on the difficulties of navigating predominantly White institutions, confronting their histories of exclusion, and charting sustainable and encouraging paths toward equity.

Restoration and rejuvenation are even more important in our lives, which is one motivation for my fun and enlightening partnership with Dr. Lisa B. Thompson on the podcast and radio segment, *Black Austin Matters*, for KUT Public Radio. This confounding and dystopian moment has inspired creativity and a rededication to the iterations of justice many of us deeply believe in, and it's what motivates me to persist in the work, and indeed find joy in working with students, staff, faculty, administrators, and people in our community.

In this narrative, I've presented a more granular perspective on my career and pathway to my work as a scholar and administrator focused on embracing diversity and equity. I have attempted to share the momentary setbacks, confusion, and liminality that many reading this have experienced, and to express that this is inherently part of the work. The goal, however, is to give a road map of one career—perhaps resembling yours, or quite different. Nevertheless, I suspect you might better understand my inspiration for studying developmental relationships, and the role of humility conjoined with achievement.

CHAPTER TWO

The Mentoring Matrix

Developmental Relationships and How They Sustain BIPOC Students, Staff, and Faculty

MENTORING HAS EMERGED as a cornerstone of many institutional DEI efforts—ensuring that members of historically underrepresented and marginalized communities have access to nurturing developmental relationships. Whether focused on programmatic interventions or specifically focused on individual students/staff/faculty, it seems mentorship has been a continual investment of time and resources. In this chapter, I leverage my own research in mentoring in higher education and my knowledge of the prevailing literature to first center mentoring, along with other developmental relationships, as a central component to creating environments that are welcoming and supportive to underrepresented students, staff, and faculty. I will then posit that an understanding of how developmental relationships are nurtured and evolve is a key component of their success, and present foundational aspects of how such approaches can work (planning, assessment, and constant access to feedback).

I'll also introduce a new term from my work, *mentorability*, which discusses how junior participants in mentoring relationships are introduced to the ways in which they can leverage access and engagement with a senior person. While there is often a justified and necessary focus on training mentors, I have found that we spend less time instructing mentees on how to best navigate their relationships so they can achieve their goals. To close the chapter, I will reflect on aspects of successful mentoring arrangements while presenting cautions and the need to examine the dynamics of mentoring relationships to avoid exploitation, abuse, and other forms of harm that are a rarely discussed, but nevertheless important aspect of developmental relationships.

WHAT IS MENTORING, EXACTLY?

My study of mentoring started as a graduate student, when I first encountered Kathy Kram's scholarship on developmental relationships.[1] Kram's work on organizational change focused on how those from underrepresented and marginalized populations—largely women and people of color—fared in organizational contexts where they were historically excluded. Kram, as well as David Thomas, noted that these individuals, despite having impeccable credentials and preparation for their roles, often were overlooked and lacked access to the "fast track" to organizational leadership and success.[2] Those access points were typically veiled and opaque; what was essential was a guide or copilot to illuminate and elucidate a way forward.

Daniel Levinson's *Seasons of a Man's Life* similarly posited that men at a certain level in organization leadership at some point turned their focus from moving up to looking back to assist those ascending organizational structures. These men, Levinson argued, are the ones most likely to be able to serve as mentors to those new in the organization—with an ambition no longer oriented toward competition, they instead invested their energy in advancing those with promise as a way of securing their legacy.[3] Around the same time I read these books about mentoring as an emerging educational researcher in my doctoral program, I encountered the concept of the *hidden curriculum*—the aspects, routines, jargon, and behaviors embedded in organizational contexts that those inside and in leadership understood but were veiled and foreign to newcomers.[4]

As a first-generation collegian and permanent new kid in my formative years, I was all too aware of this phenomenon. My favorite example of this is from my first year in college. I had class in a rather large lecture hall at the University of Texas right after lunch, and I rushed to get to the classroom before the bell. I found myself in the middle of the lecture hall, and sure enough about fifteen minutes in, I needed to use the restroom. The professor was midlecture, and it seemed impossibly rude to just get up as she was talking. Additionally, I was in the middle of the room so I couldn't subtly slide out. After minutes of mental machinations, I realized I needed to act to save my bladder. I raised my hand . . . and the professor continued to lecture. *So now what?* I kept my hand up until the professor looked at me exasperatedly and said, "Yes? What is it?" I asked to be excused to the restroom . . . to a look of incredulity. She said, "Yes, of course." The classroom was silent, then tittering laughter began. I was too uncomfortable to care, but as I returned, I realized I'd transgressed—forever known as The Dude Who Asked to Use the Restroom. I tell this story to my students today, because I realize many of them haven't been told how high school differs from college—where it's acceptable to discreetly leave a classroom for any reason. I went to an inner-city high school, where leaving a classroom without permission had serious consequences. This story usually gets a few nervous laughs, and that's fine—I've established that I am a human being and that there are unwritten rules and policies that I'm happy to make plain to my students.

UNPACKING THE HIDDEN CURRICULUM

The hidden curriculum is a secret code that all those in the organization hold, but you're initially oblivious to the fact it exists. Eventually, from your experience of not fitting in, you become aware that something's happening. There are conversations, instructions, and shortcuts you're not privy to, but others are. Those in the in group start to advance and move ahead, while you stay in the same place. Being denied access to the hidden curriculum is corrosive—because while you may initially note that the marginalization is externally focused, at some point, you start to question your own knowledge, efficacy, and worth. Perhaps you're not in the loop because you're not smart enough or good enough to be successful. Eventually this leads to a sense of hopelessness—you abandon the organization, or settle for a survival existence.

But another possibility exists. Someone in the organization takes an interest in you, and starts to translate and explain the mores and ways of this foreign world. Slowly, the jargon becomes comprehensible. The subtleties of organizational life become transparent. You are now "in the loop." Your initial access point introduces you to more organizational players, and you are now able to make decisions that can move your career and interests forward. You can also opt to not engage in the activities that might propel your advancement, but at least you're making an active choice in the matter. We all get to make decisions regarding how we choose to navigate careers—but's it's hardly a decision if you're unaware of what's going on.

In essence, this is the opportunity that Kram, Thomas, and Levinson posit that mentoring relationships offer. The hidden curriculum isn't equally opaque—having aspects of one's identity that are congruent with those who are in the dominant group can provide access. I noticed this as my classmates who attended elite prep schools were more comfortable with and trusting of the adults in the college realm. They knew what to call professors and administrators, whereas I usually defaulted to the most formal title out of fear of offending someone. Membership in the dominant group—conveyed by an accent, style of dress, dropping the right names in conversation, and so on—represents a key to the curriculum. More insidious are those factors that can't be learned or accessed—our racial and ethnic identity, sexual orientation and gender identity/presentation, body size, ability status, and so forth. For those of us who hold multiple marginalized identities, the hidden curriculum rests on a higher, less accessible shelf compared to many of our peers.

The good news is that once we're aware of the hidden curriculum, we can strategize on ways to access it. We can further decide how valid and needed it is for our goals. We can additionally choose to resist or rebel against some aspects of the hidden curriculum. I was made acutely aware of the importance of drawing this distinction when I taught a course on organizational behavior in my second year at UT Austin. I had survived the first prep of the course and now felt I had the right readings and assignments to effectively teach the course. I'd even arranged for a new classroom with movable desks so students could engage in group work.

A few days in, I noticed that one of my students was constantly talking with his classmates during my presentations. Initially this was fine . . . until it became a daily occurrence. Now I was becoming annoyed and decided to confront him, which wasn't terribly difficult—Bradley was smart and affable, and we had a good relationship. After class, I pulled him aside and asked him how class was going. Bradley said it was going well and he enjoyed the class—which prompted me to ask, "So why are you often in discussion with folks at your table when I'm presenting?" Bradley laughed and said, "Dr. Reddick, lots of our class are international students. You sometimes drop cultural references into your lecture and they have no idea what you're talking about. I'm explaining what your references are about."

I was embarrassed but thankful for Bradley's transparency. Without knowing it, I was inadvertently adding pages to the hidden curriculum. This led me to institute two changes: first, I was more mindful of my cultural references (which were not just US-centric, but sometimes specific to the 1980s and 1990s—also a period that over time, fewer of my students knew), and second, I started the class with a reading from Beykont and Daiute that examines inclusive practices in a graduate school of education from the perspective of international students.[5] In the article, students discuss how American students are more comfortable "thinking out loud" and formulating perspectives on readings, which is often a direct contradiction to the way that students from other nations are asked to engage with material. As you might imagine, we would then have a robust discussion on what our formative classroom experiences were, and how we could find a common way to engage in our classroom given our diverse pathways to the learning space. This exercise became a valuable lesson in exposing my own contributions to the hidden curriculum.

MENTORING TOWARD TRANSPARENCY: RECOGNIZING CRITICAL SUPPORT FOR THE HISTORICALLY MARGINALIZED

Mentoring, and the array of developmental relationships (including role modeling, sponsorship, and coaching), can provide access to knowledge and pathways in complex organizations such as a college or university setting. While we often focus our thoughts on mentoring and supporting students, it's important to think about mentoring ecologies—someone who is a mentee is likely to be a mentor in another context. Mentoring and developmental relationships can emerge organically from common interests and connections, but they are more likely to thrive in institutional contexts where mentoring is embraced as a worthwhile activity by those who mentor and their mentees. Institutions that incorporate mentoring narratives in their presentation, on multiple levels (students, faculty, staff, community members, administrators), and those that recognize and reward exemplary mentoring via awards and academies are conveying their commitment and support of developmental relationships.

I can share an example of such recognition that I'm quite familiar with. In 2019, UT Austin launched the Provost's Distinguished Service Academy (DSA), which "represents a formal organization of distinguished tenured and senior professional-track faculty members with extraordinary achievements across their portfolios and in particular in terms of their excellence in mentoring and service to their college, the university, the state of Texas and the nation."[6] Designed to replicate the distinction and honor from research and teaching academies, this represents one of the ways that mentoring and commitment to developmental relationships can be recognized.

I first heard this idea from Dr. Nancy Cantor, chancellor of Rutgers University-Newark. At the 2016 Keeping Our Faculty of Color Symposium at the University of Minnesota, Cantor expressed her frustration that service was often relegated to the status of the least important aspect of faculty life—and that excellence in service, which she suggested calling "intramural teaching and research," should also be recognized as institutions do for excellence in teaching and research. Three years later, I was inducted with my colleagues Drs. Carolyn Brown, Jen Moon, Lisa Moore, and Loriene Roy into the UT Austin Academy. Unsurprisingly, we all knew each other, either from working together or by reputation—and we all represented marginalized identities in the academy (BIPOC, Native American, women, LGBTQ+, to name a few). Our activities include creating resources to facilitate mentoring across campus and working collaboratively to promote mentoring and service in academia through presentations, videos, and public scholarship. Further, our contributions are recognized with a stipend, just like the research and teaching academies have. There's nothing like committing financial resources to values you prioritize, and this is precisely what the Distinguished Service Academy portends.

CREATE A PROGRAM OR LET A THOUSAND MENTORING RELATIONSHIPS BLOOM: WHAT'S THE BEST APPROACH?

I am often asked if I support formalized mentoring programs targeted toward underrepresented populations (BIPOC, women, and first-gen, for instance), or if it's better to create informal mentoring networks without the imprimatur of a program. I respond by saying *both* approaches are needed and necessary—but navigating a large bureaucratic institution, with its silos and peculiarities, can be difficult, which is where formal mentoring programs come in. Mentoring programs that are staffed to facilitate matching of mentors and mentees, provide training and support to all involved, and create accountability systems and interventions if mentoring arrangements go awry represent some of the better approaches to supporting a healthy mentoring ecosystem.

However, it is important to provide flexibility in matching and expectations: I spoke to a student who related to me that the two mentoring programs he was a part of expected him to maintain a steady schedule of meetings and check-ins with his mentors, which he found overwhelming. In addition to the structure and assessment of efforts that a formal mentoring program can provide, however, members of our community should be encouraged to seek out developmental relationships in different aspects of their academic and professional journeys. Institutions can provide opportunities for members of the community to find each other—research colloquia, convenings around work-life balance, and career-oriented affinity groups that leverage community and alumni expertise are some ways to ensure that the developmental relationship soil is nurtured.

The Importance of Homophily—When It's Possible

Existing and thriving in an institutional context in which one infrequently encounters stories of success from members of one's community can be exceedingly challenging. Furthermore, there are some experiences that may be uniquely understood or appreciated by people with the same identity membership. We call such mentoring arrangements *homophilous*, and this is a concern I often hear vocalized by people in underrepresented identity groups—Asian American women find a special bond and understanding with other Asian American women, and so forth.[7] I understand, appreciate, and champion these needs, which I have drawn upon throughout my own life. But what happens when there are very few in the institution who hold that identity? I can posit a few solutions.

First, technology has expanded the possibilities of developmental relationships, including mentoring. Johnson described "e-mentoring" as a valid developmental relationship, and the global pandemic of 2020 has forced many scholars and practitioners to become familiar with technologies such as Zoom, Microsoft Teams, and Google Hangouts, to name a few.[8] Suddenly, the options available for mentorship have increased. Social media, particularly Twitter and Instagram, have provided a platform for many communities to find each other virtually, creating the potential for what I have termed "mentors-at-a-distance"—with an understanding that the parameters and depth of connection are entirely up to the parties involved.[9]

Indeed, sometimes the episodic and novel nature of mentoring-at-a-distance is a value that makes the relationship unique. Furthermore, the possibility of building an impactful relationship that may transform into face-to-face meetings exists; I know of mentoring dyads where the participants meet up at conferences annually or whenever they find they are in proximity to one another. I'm reminded of a story I heard from a Black woman computer scientist, who shared that her peer group of Black women computer scientists remains close through technology and an annual meetup at a conference they all attend. I think a key aspect of this is that there should be no judgment about the nature of the relationship (in-person vs. virtual, episodic vs. frequent) if it works for both individuals.

Second, I believe that mentoring is a type of relationship that should be frequent in the lives of people. There is a tendency to believe that mentorship is between two people in a dyad, when in fact, mentoring, like friendship, should take multiple forms. Dr. Kerry Ann Rockquemore, through her work with the National Center for Faculty Development and Diversity, has created a mentoring map, which places you in the center with categories radiating out from the middle—role models, accountability partners, access to opportunities, sponsorship, substantive feedback, professional development, emotional support, intellectual community, and safe space.[10]

The goal is to identify people who slot into these categories, which means that the empty slots are spaces where one might consider seeking or building a connection. This connects to the concept of constellation mentoring, which is often called the "board of directors" approach—just as any corporation or nonprofit has a CEO who is advised by a board, one can conceptualize their professional and academic journey as being informed by a personal board of directors.[11] In this model, members of the board/constellation bring different strengths and sources of knowledge to drawn on. At times, the mentee can consult with the board/constellation members for a broad array of recommendations and advice. One of the more interesting aspects of mentorship I hear about from senior partners in dyads is that they are sometimes fearful and overwhelmed with the responsibility of being the sole person their mentee is accessing for advice—in fact, many mentors are able to give more honest and direct advice if they know their mentee is soliciting perspectives from others.

Last, sometimes it is worthwhile and important to seek nonhomophilous mentors. The field of cross-identity mentoring relationships has expanded in recent years due to two related phenomena: a lack of representation among some identity groups in higher education, and cultural taxation. Let's take the representation issue first.

The National Center for Education Statistics (NCES) can provide data regarding our faculty diversity across the nation. First, out of 1.5 million faculty in degree-granting postsecondary institutions, 54% are full time. That means 46% of postsecondary faculty are part time—which might suggest they may not have the time or resources to commit to mentoring students, though it's a certainty that many do. But if we look at the 54% who are working full time, the racial breakdown is stunning: 75% are White (40% males, 35% females), 12% are Asian/Pacific Islanders (7% males, 5% females), 6% are Black (3% males, 3% females), 6% are Hispanic (3% males, 3% females), 1% are American Indian/Alaska Native, and 1% are two or more races (NCES, 2020).[12]

Compare with the breakdown of all students in degree-granting postsecondary institutions in 2019: 54% White (23% males, 31% females), 13% Black (5% males, 8% females), 20% Hispanic (8% males, 12% females), 7% Asian/Pacific Islander (3% males, 4% females), 0.7% American Indian/Alaska Native (0.3% male, 0.4% female), and 4% two or more races (2% male, 2% female).[13] *Simply put, the numbers on the faculty side demonstrate a paucity of same-race mentors for BIPOC students.* Furthermore, the unique challenges of being a BIPOC faculty member, which can include additional, uncompensated work to support diversity and community engagement—cultural taxation—also means the available time and energy for mentoring relationships may not be the same as compared to White faculty mentors.[14]

STRATEGIES FOR EFFECTIVE CROSS-IDENTITY MENTORING

This might sound like bad news for emerging BIPOC students (and staff and faculty). In fact, there is a promising approach with cross-race mentoring relationships. Thomas's early work on cross-race mentoring posited the need for congruity among mentoring dyads when it came to the role of race in the mentee's ascent in an organization—if a mentor and mentee have a common belief about how racial identity factors in their advancement (or lack thereof), they can agree and strategize about how to negotiate these challenges. However, if the mentor is race avoidant, and the mentee is race conscious, it's easy to see how this will be a major impediment in the relationship (and vice versa).[15] But even with congruity about how race matters (or doesn't matter), is that enough to produce positive cross-race mentoring dyads?

In my research on White faculty mentors of Black undergraduate students, I observed a pattern of experiences among the mentors that they themselves frequently had not. As a researcher who employs phenomenological methods, I asked the mentors about their formative experiences, well before they became faculty members. Each of them related a story—or multiple stories—of experiencing marginalization firsthand or witnessing such experiences with someone they were close to. Sometimes the incidents were deeply embedded in the mentors' family history: some reflected on a family trajectory impacted by anti-Semitism and the Holocaust, while others shared immigration histories where previous generations came to the US and experienced discrimination and xenophobia.

These incidents were relayed in the stories parents and grandparents passed along to the mentors, as well as their faith and civic commitments. For other mentors, more immediate and personal examples of marginalization came forth. Having a sibling negotiating the experience of coming out and being the sole source of support impacted one of my study participants. Another mentor shared how his relationship with his spouse, a woman scientist, exposed him secondhand to the casual sexism and misogyny she experienced from her postdoctoral studies to her professional career: "So when a student tells me they experienced racism, I tend to believe them."

Another poignant example is when a mentor shared the experience of going to a restaurant he had frequented alone and with White friends, but in this instance with a Black woman friend. That particular instance, the pair waited for an extended time to be seated, something the mentor had never experienced before. He recounted this episode with a great deal of emotion—he certainly knew that racism existed, but he was witnessing it firsthand, realizing his Black woman companion suffered such indignities on a regular basis. For another mentor I interviewed, it was the experience of growing up in Scandinavia as a Western European. Casual teasing, and even his accented language, made him acutely aware of his difference from his peers. He related this to his mindset when he made note of Black students in his courses: "I can appreciate that by virtue of being one of a small number, or the only student of their race, that they might need to know that I am aware of the dynamic, and they might be in need of a little care."[16]

PROXIMAL EXPERIENCES OF BEING OTHERED: AN EMPATHETIC BRIDGE TOWARD CROSS-IDENTITY MENTORSHIP

I call this phenomenon *proximal experiences of being othered.*[17] In these mentors' personal lives, they have witnessed the emotional intensity and pain of being ostracized. Such experiences have heightened their empathetic responses, and in some ways they can better relate to what someone who is a member of an underrepresented identity group might be experiencing. I must state that this is not as simple as saying, "I've been oppressed, so my oppression is equal (or worse!) than yours." I think it's fairly evident that such a perspective would have a corrosive impact on a mentoring relationship. Instead, the effect is more like a "Spidey sense" that their mentee is potentially navigating daily microaggressive challenges in their environment—and these mentors tend to *validate* these experiences rather than overlook or dismiss them. Or worse yet, excuse transgressive assaults on their identity: "I'm sure that wasn't racism; perhaps they were just having a bad day."

Along with this understanding was a respect and admiration for their mentees being both resistant and resilient to the daily indignities they deflected. Proximal experiences of being othered tend to be implicit, operating on a subconscious level. None of the mentors I interviewed volunteered, "I'm able to effectively mentor across race because something relatable happened to me." Rather, these stories emerged after hours of examining their own formative experiences, often accompanied by moments of contemplation, sighs, and even tears. It seems to me that by mining one's own experiences—and relating to the pain and indignity of being marginalized—there are building blocks of empathy on which one can construct a practice of validating and supporting someone traveling a pathway obstructed by microaggressions and racism. While my research looked expressly at racism, I feel that proximal experiences of being othered can be leveraged to support mentees confronting sexism, homophobia, ableism, classism, and a variety of intersecting oppressions—with the strong caveat that while these lived experiences can provide some knowledge and intuition, they are not the same as what the mentee is experiencing.

HOW DO WE KNOW IT'S WORKING? ASSESSING MENTORING RELATIONSHIPS

I'm sometimes asked how to assess the impact of a mentoring relationship. My colleague and fellow mentoring researcher Dr. Gloria Crisp has created the College Student Mentoring Scale that measures students' perceptions of the mentoring support they receive in college.[18] Along with this scale, I tend to believe that interviews can inform what is working in the relationship. Asking for ways that the mentoring relationship has informed and inspired actions toward one's goals, how both mentor and mentee perceive the importance and engagement of the relationship to themselves as well as their partner, and if they find value in the relationship are important topics to investigate.

Mentors and mentees are human, so understanding how the pair have overcome (or are working to overcome) challenges is also significant. Last, ensuring that the relationship is healthy and welcoming of other forms of support and development, including other mentoring relationships, and that both mentee and mentor have spaces of support beyond this particular relationship is essential. Like all intimate relationships, the potential for well-intentioned mentoring to take a turn toward toxicity exists, and both mentee and mentor need to be able to assess the value of and contributions to their relationship free from threat or fear of negative repercussions from one another.

Ultimately, I think one of the best ways of assessing a mentoring relationship is for each partner to ask themselves, "Do I find this relationship rewarding and worthwhile? If so, why? And if not, what's not working?" and then to share their reflections with each other. Social exchange theory posits that the mentor-mentee relationship is predicated on equilibrium, expectancy, and the distribution of justice in the pairing.[19] Simply put, if there is a persistent imbalance between what a mentor and a mentee put into the relationship, the relationship is likely to end.

DISCOVERING MENTORABILITY

At the time I was starting my own scholarly inquiry on mentoring under the guidance of Dr. Stacy Blake-Beard, Boston-based scholars such as Dr. Jean Rhodes and others at the Harvard School of Public Health, alongside community agencies such as MENTOR and Big Brothers Big Sisters, advocated for the declaration of a National Mentoring Month. In 2002, President George W. Bush proclaimed January as the first National Mentoring Month, and subsequently President Barack Obama continued this legacy, as the My Brother's Keeper initiative became one of his administration's cornerstone programs.[20] As an emerging researcher in this area, I was excited that mentoring had captured the national attention in such a way, and more frequently found myself giving talks and workshops each January (which also coincided with the Dr. Martin Luther King, Jr. holiday, whose life and example contained many powerful developmental relationships). I began to notice that I was often talking with organizations that had large-scale mentoring programs—they eagerly embraced the importance of developmental relationships, but were trying to make these programs more effective. How could they engage mentees more effectively, especially across race, age, and socioeconomic status?

It was a dilemma I puzzled over for some time, including my own bond with the UT Austin service organization Texas Blazers, who mentored young people at my alma mater, Johnston High School in Austin. A few years later in 2012, I was honored with the Outstanding Young Texas Ex Award along with Ben De Leon, who was additionally recognized as the 2009 National Big Brother of the Year. In conversations with Ben and the Blazers, and a multitude of mentoring program directors, I began to think more about how much emphasis we were placing on mentors via training and workshops. Yet I could barely recall what information was being conveyed to mentees. Often it was a vague admonition that they were getting a mentor, that it would be a good thing, and to follow the policies (meeting with the mentor, primarily).

It was then that I got a call from Dr. David Perez II, a good friend and colleague who chaired the Association for the Study of Higher Education (ASHE) Council on Ethnic Participation (CAHEP) Pre-Conference Mentoring Program. The idea was to have new members—primarily graduate students—link with a mentor at the ASHE Conference, our subdiscipline's largest convening. David asked me to keynote the address to the mentees at the November 2014 conference in Washington, DC, and I eagerly agreed. I thought of this as an opportunity to create a toolkit for mentees to make their mentoring relationships more impactful.

I reached out to my circle of scholar friends who were working in the area of mentoring and also effective mentors: Drs. Vicki Baker, Marybeth Gasman, Kimberly Griffin, and Frank Tuitt. What advice, I asked, would they pass along to those about to embark on a mentoring journey? More pointedly, I asked them—What should mentees know about your commitments, values, and concerns about being a mentor?

The second question gave me some of the most interesting responses: the importance of checking in on a regular basis, following through and being open to constructive criticism, understanding that mentors were balancing multiple obligations and needed direction from mentees, and understanding mentoring as a two-way street for mentees and mentors. It then dawned on me—we needed a user's guide for mentees to maximize the beneficial aspects of the mentoring game. I thought about a term I'd often hear in sports, "being coachable." A coachable player is one who is receptive and responsive to coaching—so perhaps a mentee who is receptive and responsive to mentoring is . . . *mentorable?*

I was convinced that someone had already put the term into the academic marketplace—but while I did find references to "mentor ability," nothing came up in my searches. So I titled my keynote at the ASHE CAHEP meeting "Mentorability: Navigating Developmental Relationships."[21] At the end of the talk, I spent a lot of time talking with conference attendees, who shared that this was the first time they'd been advised on how to utilize the mentoring dyad. Returning to Austin, I shared the feedback with my PhD advisee Laura Struve, and we put together an unpublished white paper detailing what exactly "mentorability" was.[22] We were framing mentorability not in the sense of what mentors could do for mentees, but what junior people interested in a developmental relationship could do to attract a caring and effective mentor.

The Tenets of Mentorability

We came up with three pillars from what our mentoring experts had shared: (1) putting in what you intend to get, (2) thought partnership, and (3) seeing beyond homophily. "Putting in what you intend to get" is an accessible way of saying "reciprocity." I recalled my interviews with mentors and an article I had written with colleagues Drs. Rick Cherwitz and Kimberly Griffin.[23] We kept hearing mentors, with a slight sense of sheepishness, relate how they felt they were getting more from the relationship than their mentee—*Was that okay?* I recalled a conversation with Ben De Leon recounting how his Little Brother might have taught him more, rather than the other way around. Indeed, one of my mentees, Andrew Limmer, shared a similar reflection about his mentee at Johnston High. Laura and I explained the concept thus:

> Oftentimes, mentees see mentoring as something that is done for them, rather than an organic, functioning relationship in which they need to contribute equally. Some exasperated mentors share that their mentees don't respond to emails, calls, or texts in a timely fashion. This leaves a mentor feeling rejected and unimportant—not a good way to encourage investment in a relationship. Mentors and mentees should agree from the outset about how and how often they

> will communicate, and even how they will communicate that they're too busy to engage at the moment! It sounds simple, but this aspect of mentorability is often overlooked.[24]

"Thought partnership" was our way of framing mentoring as a collaboration requiring contributions from mentee and mentor. In our work, mentors expressed a desire for reciprocity and the fear that mentees expect them to be the only ones to provide work and life advice, something they found quite intimidating. This responsibility for directing someone's major life decisions could lead the mentor to retreat, not engage. In our view, mentorship works best when mentees do two things: one, come to the relationship with their own ideas, looking for guidance rather than expecting a mentor to tell them what to do; and two, find a constellation of mentors and advisors to guide their paths. To paraphrase a familiar saying, it wouldn't be inappropriate to suggest that it takes a constellation to mentor someone.

"Seeing beyond homophily" goes back to the dilemma often presented to BIPOC students in predominantly White institutions. There may not be mentors of their racial and ethnic identity available (and those who are present are often stretched thin and can't take on massive mentoring loads), so what should they do? While we believe it is very important to find mentors that have encountered similar experiences, it's also important to develop mentoring relationships beyond our tendency to associate and bond with similar others. We were reminded of Marybeth Gasman's simple but resonant statement in a *Washington Post* editorial: "White faculty need to step up."[25] Scholars such as Drs. David Thomas, Audrey Murrell, and Stacy Blake-Beard have examined the potential strengths and pitfalls of cross-race mentoring, and the most salient characteristic of strong mentoring can be summarized in the words of a mentor I once interviewed: "Ultimately, it's about love."[26] Effective mentorship is based on a deep-rooted concern and care for all parties involved, which can transcend identity markers—with forethought and intentionality (recall the concept of proximal experiences of being othered).

MENTORABILITY GAINS VISIBILITY

Laura and I never published that paper—we had some other publications that were taking up our time—but we continued to talk about it. During one of those discussions, two new doctoral students, Victoria Black and Zach Taylor, decided to further extend mentorability into presentations at the National Mentoring Conference at the University of New Mexico, and into a publication.[27] Victoria, in particular, found mentorability to be useful in her role as director of peer mentoring in the PACE program at Texas State University. I later learned that Victoria had first heard me talk about mentorability at the Texas Mentoring Conference in San Antonio in 2016, and her own dissertation deeply examined how we prepare and support mentees navigating their developmental relationships. In 2018, Victoria presented an incredible TED talk entitled "No One is Talking to the Mentees," which does a first-rate job of presenting the pillars of mentorability.[28] It's received over 35,000 views to date.

Victoria starts her talk by describing one of her first and most important relationships with a mentor named Susan, and shares how as a first-gen student, she appreciated their cultural connection and Susan's personal interest in her development. But she asked herself, "Was I a good mentee? Did I know what to expect, how to engage, and what was my responsibility?" Victoria challenges the thought that mentorship is one way, declaring it "so much more that." In the research Victoria conducted with Zach Taylor, they looked at 187 mentoring programs in four-year public institutions in Texas and found that websites were four times more likely to address mentor responsibilities than those of mentees. Victoria further notes that if programs are assessed on the development of mentees, we're not doing a good job on what to expect—because *nobody's talking to the mentees.*

Victoria issues a challenge to the audience to transform their next relationship, noting that mentorability is the willingness to understand that "we grow from others as others grow from us," with three components: commitment (being physically and mentally present), reciprocity (initiative taking, knowing what you bring to the relationship, and partnership), and vulnerability (accepting and embracing change). Victoria closes her talk with a word cloud that she assembled over the years presenting across the country on mentorability in response to the question, "What is the one attribute that mentees can bring to the relationship?" The most frequently cited terms are "open minded" and "vulnerable."

She then asks the audience to ask themselves three questions: (1) Are you committed and willing to make time for the partnership? (2) Do you understand the reciprocity you bring to the relationship? and (3) Are you truly willing to be open minded and vulnerable to change? Urging the audience to "reimagine our commitment as mentees," Victoria urges us to "live [our] own mentorability." Even today, watching the TED talk gives me goosebumps as the now Dr. Victoria Black brings the concept to an audience in such an accessible and clear manner. I'm grateful for her critical contributions and insights on mentorability.[29]

CONFRONTING THE UNCOMFORTABLE: WHEN MENTORING RELATIONSHIPS GO SOUTH

There's a commendable body of research on mentoring and other developmental relationships, so I think it's high time we moved from the rather empty declarations of "mentoring magic." In fact, we can identify many of the best practices in mentoring, detailed in this chapter. That isn't to say that there aren't still mysteries in what makes relationships click—the uniqueness and quirkiness of our personalities can offset a lot of what seems to be workable and effective. This is why I always advocate for an "escape hatch" for relationships, especially for those that are parts of structured programs. Both mentees and mentors should be able to approach a program administrator to explain that a relationship may not have come together in a manner that is conducive for either party. It may mean that the pairing is better suited for role modeling, sponsorship, or another relationship—or no relationship at all. Both parties have a responsibility to acknowledge that the relationship might be beyond repair.

There is a particular responsibility that mentors have, and that is not to engage in exploitation and abuse in the relationship. Because the boundaries of mentoring can blend into other types of relationships (such as friendships), the former is sometimes hard to discern. It's even tackled in one of my favorite episodes of the classic sitcom *Seinfeld*, "The Fatigues."

> GEORGE: I still don't understand this. Abby has a mentor?
> JERRY: Yes. And the mentor advises the protégé.
> GEORGE: Is there any money involved?
> JERRY: No.
> GEORGE: So what's in it for the mentor?
> JERRY: Respect, admiration, prestige.
> GEORGE: Pssh. Would the protégé pick up stuff for the mentor?
> JERRY: I suppose if it was on the protégé's way to the mentor, they might.
> GEORGE: Laundry? Dry cleaning?
> JERRY: It's not a *valet*, it's a *protégé*.[30]

Jerry's information is mostly accurate—I would be wary of any request that exploits positional power. Would a mentee willingly say, "I prefer not to pick up your things," without fear of retribution? If the response is unclear, it's best to stay away from it. Peer relationships are the best ways to "pick up stuff," it seems.

Addressing Hierarchy and Power in Mentoring Relationships

Mentors need to be particularly aware of power dynamics in a developmental relationship—and rather than pretending they're unimportant, do what they can to eliminate the distance and acknowledge where the distance cannot be brokered. As an example, I make it clear to my doctoral advisees (who often become my mentees as we work on research and writing projects) that the fact that I am responsible for assigning an evaluative grade in coursework means I have a particular responsibility to ensure they know what those expectations are—this should not be clouded by a working relationship or affection for each other. Fortunately, most of the time we are working together because of a shared interest and proven commitment to the work. A useful technique to employ is to ask yourself, "What would I say if I was a mentee in this situation, and *didn't* want to do what I'm asking them to do?" If you have a sense that the answer is influenced by not wanting to disappoint the mentor, it's a question perhaps better not asked.

Abuse and Exploitation in Mentoring Relationships

More concerning is the potential for abuse in mentoring relationships. For all the good we can see in mentoring, the intimate nature of the relationship can sometimes obfuscate clear boundaries. Popular media often casts the (typically female, typically younger) ingenue in a relationship with the (typically older, typically male) guide—and it turns romantic. Such a change in the relationship has to be done explicitly, openly, and with a clear understanding of the consequences (and I should note, most institutions have explicit guidelines about intimate relationships between individuals who have supervisory or organizational responsibility over their partner). A romantic or close personal relationship can end, and if it does, it may likely mean the end of the developmental relationship. Are both parties aware, and mindful of this, and the position the other member of the dyad might find themselves in?

Fairly or unfairly, mentoring relationships are apparent in organizational contexts, and the perception of the dynamic is an aspect that must be negotiated. Assumptions about the nature of the relationship can be thorny and embarrassing to discuss. I always advocate for transparency—it should be known to all in the organization that you are mentoring and being mentored (and hopefully, in multiple developmental relationships). A good question to ask is, "Would I engage in the same activities and settings with another mentee of a different race/ethnicity/faith system/gender/sexual orientation/ability status?" If the answer is no, it's good to ask why.

CROSS-GENDER MENTORING IN THE #METOO ERA: A CALL TO "LEAN IN" TO APPROPRIATE MENTORING RELATIONSHIPS

In 2019, I was disturbed by a report in the *New York Times* about a session at the Davos Forum where several men expressed anxieties about mentoring women.[31] No doubt, the repercussions of the #MeToo movement, in which more than two hundred prominent men have been removed from their positions, influenced this discussion. #MeToo seems to have provoked concerns that cross-identity, and in particular, cross-gender mentoring should be approached with caution.

I find this view conflates the serious issue of harassment with boundary setting. Impactful mentoring should be *cognizant* of gender identity, but not limited by it. In so many organizational settings, the only mentorship available to junior women is from men—which is why I find the thought of men shying away from mentoring women so troubling. If some men withdraw from mentoring, this impacts the ability of women to advance in leadership—particularly for BIPOC women who often experience intersectional marginalization in organizations that are male dominated and predominantly White.

Acknowledging Intimacy, Appropriately

Mentoring, by definition, is a close relationship between a junior person and a senior person in an organization and can't be done at arm's length. Other types of developmental relationships, such as role modeling, sponsorship, and coaching, are less personal and intimate. Mentoring, of course, connects career development and personal development. The match between mentor and mentee matters, personality and interest-wise—so not just anyone can mentor another. We also know from the work of researchers such as Dr. Rosabeth Moss Kanter that it is also unlikely that women leaders will emerge without the support and nurturing of supportive mentors.[32]

Toxic masculinity, which is the socially sanctioned behavior of men that validates aggression and status climbing (and not men themselves), is a significant cause of this dysfunction—sometimes manifesting itself in the workplace, where some men feel their everyday interactions with women are so at risk of accusations of harassment that they resolve to avoid women altogether. (Think of former vice president Mike Pence's "never dine alone with a woman" rule.)[33]

However, I argue that it's entirely possible to develop close, supportive relationships entirely devoid of harassment. Organizational leaders must reckon with the ethics of what it means for some to "opt out" of any engagement with women; this essentially embraces the idea that men are unable to control their behavior or lack judgment about what constitutes appropriate conduct—an affront to the professionalism and obligations of men in the organization. It would be inappropriate for anyone to purposely avoid a colleague out of fear of a false accusation of impropriety; however, we have social attitudes that term men of color (particularly Black men) as hypersexual and aggressive. These tropes and stereotypes should be addressed by hearing the narratives of men of color who have experienced such harm. However, simply reifying this choice is the essence of a mindset that limits the potential for mentorship across gender identities.[34]

I posit that there is a bright line between supportive mentoring and harassment: sharing work projects and interpersonal networks, and identifying strengths and weaknesses in a résumé should not trigger a response in male mentors to retreat. Men who mentor junior women have a responsibility to ensure their protégés are protected and treated as they would want to be treated: as emerging leaders, as valued members of the organization who bring impressive skills to work, and as equals in potential and aspirations.

All organizations should embrace gender equity as a goal. If leaders employ strategies such as training and role-playing over mentoring situations that can become problematic, and raise awareness of impediments such as toxic masculinity, they can inform mentors and mentees of ways to successfully navigate relationships. Indeed, it is incredibly informative and important that cross-gender groups discuss the dynamics of and challenges in the experiences of women aspiring to leadership so we can eradicate these pathologies.[35]

CROSS-IDENTITY MENTORING IN AN ERA OF RACIAL RECKONING

Similarly, I have heard some concerns from White people in university settings who express trepidation in working closely with BIPOC communities out of fear of being "canceled," with the moment of racial reckoning inspired in the wake of the murders of George Floyd, Breonna Taylor, Tony McDade, and Ahmaud Arbery in 2020. This might be more accurately illustrated as a moment to consider how some behaviors and language are being (rightly) questioned—I'm mindful of a number of recent situations in US public schools where Black children were punished for wearing their hair in dreadlocks and braids, and the corresponding legislative responses, such as California's CROWN Act of 2019 which prohibits discrimination based on hair style and texture.[36]

In both the fears of being accused of harassment and the fears of cancellation, we see the perspectives of those who hold power and positions of dominance in organizations override the needs and voices of those who experience marginalization. It seems only fair and just to prioritize the latter perspectives over the former—and the need for organizations to scaffold and support education and engagement to discuss how the present sociopolitical context impacts how we all approach our work and learning in institutions of higher education, and beyond.

I sense much of the problem comes when the senior person in the relationship speaks without knowing or understanding how their mentee is negotiating a sociopolitical dynamic that constantly devalues Black and BIPOC lives. This is where spending more time listening pays dividends in building trust and respect between the members of the dyad. Furthermore, it is important to develop an understanding that more empathy, rather than judgment, is needed from those who hold privileged identities. Empathy does not mean that one agrees with all the strategies and positions of another; rather, it means that there is a vested effort to understand, and to place oneself in another's shoes and take in the world from that perspective.

There should also be clear communication about what constitutes "open for discussion" aspects of the relationship and areas that at this time are best not broached. Sometimes this is because the individuals in the relationship themselves have not yet had the time or opportunity to come to terms with their own feelings on such a sensitive topic, and other times it is because the lived experience is so painfully acute, it may not feel psychologically safe to share at that moment. Instead of lamenting this seeming barrier, mentors and mentees can work to build trust and safety in other aspects of their relationship and take pride in those strengths. For all the significance of intimacy in mentoring relationships, it's perfectly fine for there to be topics that aren't shared and discussed. We have arrays of relationships where it might feel more appropriate and safer to discuss sociopolitical matters.

However, as a senior partner in a mentoring dyad, I feel there is some accountability to be responsive if the junior partner is eager and willing to discuss their concerns about existing in predominantly White spaces (as well as those that are predominantly male, cisgender, nonimmigrant, straight, middle class, etc.). I often advise mentors to do their own reading and reflecting, both in the national context and about issues that are more local. One aspect of privilege is the ability to navigate spaces without the burden of historical oppression—not reflecting on the fact that our organizations and institutions once excluded us based on our identities, often not that long ago. Knowing how historically marginalized people view their inclusion/exclusion in our spaces is a critical step in bridging the experiential divides we often have in the spaces where we work and learn.

An example of this vital space for growth occurred in June 2020, when nine of the top ten books in the *New York Times*' nonfiction bestseller list were books focused on race. Many people took the commendable step of educating themselves on how race shapes the experiences of both BIPOC and White Americans. The next step is engaging courageously in dialogue with others—particularly those who share experiences of privilege or marginalization—and formulating plans of action that have measurable steps to assess progress.

A lot of this is self-work, and should not be primarily shouldered by BIPOC, women, queer, and otherwise marginalized colleagues. In the next chapter, we'll explore how the fulcrum of diversity, equity, inclusion, and belonging work frequently is far too close to those who are historically and systemically on the periphery of our institutions. Now that you have an understanding of the role mentoring and developmental relationships play in our collective work, we can deeply examine how to acknowledge and reverse these inequities.

CHAPTER THREE

Who's Going to Take the Weight?

Navigating DEI Work While Honoring Autonomy and Balance

ALL OF THE AFOREMENTIONED aspects of creating welcoming and inclusive environments in institutions of higher education—mentoring, programming, and community engagement, to name three—require time, effort, and emotional labor from people within the organization (and at times, beyond). An essential question, then, is *who* will take on these essential and necessary responsibilities? Both the body of literature and my own personal experience and observations indicate that this work tends to gravitate toward the members of the community who hold minoritized and underrepresented identities.[1] Specifically, BIPOC individuals, women, queer-identifying individuals, people with disabilities, and those from low-income backgrounds—and those who hold intersecting identities from these populations—often assume the mantle of guiding and leading institutional efforts toward equity and inclusion.[2]

There is a logic to this. Grassroots activism within colleges and universities, as well as the communities of which they are part, often comes from historically marginalized groups. These are the folks who demand access and inclusion, create collective communities of support, and hold institutions to account.[3] The aspect that many tend to overlook is that these activists are often working from the periphery of institutions, with limited access to power and resources to effect impactful change. Again, the hidden curriculum that dictates institutional priorities and initiatives can be inaccessible, and often, the essential work of holding institutions accountable is all-consuming, resulting in dissatisfaction, distrust, fatigue, and institutional inertia.

There are problematic assumptions with the idea that diversity, equity, inclusion, and belonging work are the domain of historically marginalized communities.[4] Not everyone from an underrepresented identity group has scholarly and practical expertise in these issues; their pursuits are as varied as those that exist in the majority population. Further, this work can be emotionally intensive—and not everyone is willing to allocate their energy in such a manner. As people with socially consequential identities, oppression and bias are woven into our daily existence; for one's well-being, we must establish thresholds for how much of this corrective work on behalf of the institution we are all willing to take on.[5]

This chapter defines and gives examples of how cultural taxation negatively impacts the experiences of minoritized students, staff, and faculty at PWIs. My own work in this area of inquiry serves as the foundation and additionally challenges some of the more common remedies to cultural taxation—for example, simply not inviting those most vulnerable to cultural taxation to participate in DEI work. This chapter speaks to both those who have experienced cultural taxation, providing strategies on how to respond to culturally taxing contexts and situations, as well as those who may be inadvertently inflicting cultural taxation, challenging their framing of DEI responses and responsibility. In closing, I advance structural changes to promotion and tenure processes that institutional leaders can enact and embrace that would reduce the systemic demands of cultural taxation.

THAT KNOWING LOOK: THE EXTRA TAX MARGINALIZED PEOPLE PAY

Regardless of one's expertise and interest, people from underrepresented identities nevertheless find themselves in the work of advancing equity.[6] I know many reading this grew up with the admonition from elders, "We have to work twice as hard to go half as far." Our work must be exemplary and free from mistakes; we must maintain a sense of professionalism that exceeds our White, cis, straight, male, upper-income, and temporarily able-bodied peers; and we can never appear unwilling to take on greater responsibilities, lest we be labeled with that most pernicious of labels—*lazy*.[7] As a Black male, I have recoiled from that appellation all my life, and I suspect many reading this have as well. Perhaps this is why, even with the aforementioned caveats, people from marginalized identities still serve on committees and volunteer for projects that advance institutional equity. Whether we call it the Black tax, Brown tax, pink tax, queer tax . . . in my presentations and dialogues at selective universities, community colleges, student organizations, and alumni groups, heads nod vigorously when I ask people if they are familiar with these experiences.[8]

When I ask what these obligations and extra duties look like, I typically receive a plethora of examples. I recall one man expressing his frustration in being asked to translate Spanish documents or even recommend good Mexican restaurants—what Spivak would call being a "native informant."[9] I've had many Black professionals share how they simultaneously anticipate and abhor February—a month where they will see their culture and heritage highlighted but also know they will be tapped to serve on Black History Month committees, often serving in a cautionary role: "let's be mindful about labeling all Black people as African American, and let's be *especially* careful if we're planning a culinary event."[10]

Women will share how they are tapped to mentor new women in the organization, regardless of their job function or proximity to the new hires. For queer professionals, this is often manifested in being a walking Wikipedia about all things related to LGBTQIA+ identity—regardless of their own comfort and knowledge, and representing only their experience. I recall an awkward situation where a student asked a good friend very personal questions of a sexual nature, perhaps emboldened by his generous nature and willingness to speak to issues about politics in the gay community. I am certain we have all experienced or witnessed many cringeworthy examples in our own lives that could fill a chapter—and if these examples sound shocking, I can assure you if you ask your peers and colleagues, you'll hear many more.

Being someone who has always gravitated to equity work, it took me many years to learn (and the counsel of wise mentors) that I was not obligated to take on every issue and cause that impacted efforts for inclusion and representation. Particularly in predominantly White settings, where I was one of a few, or even the only person of color, I felt that not being involved conveyed indifference—or worse yet, a surrendering of oversight to a group that may have lacked the sensitivity to understand how an action seen as supportive could come across as tokenizing, and in fact the opposite of what was intended. Therefore, when I encountered Dr. Amado Padilla's 1994 article, "Ethnic Minority Scholars, Research, and Mentoring: Current and Future Issues" on a microfiche copy of *Educational Researcher*, I knew I had finally found a conceptual "box" to fit this tense feeling in.[11]

UNDERSTANDING CULTURAL TAXATION

Padilla's article is short—only three pages—but is probably the article I have cited the most in my scholarly career. Padilla starts by laying out the dilemma for underrepresented scholars, who have to balance the perceptions of others should they pursue research on the community of which they are part. Next, Padilla brings forth the challenges of finding mentors with cultural knowledge and cracking the code of where to publish—issues

I was grappling with as I read this as a graduate student. The last page, however, is where Padilla introduces the term *cultural taxation*—which is well fleshed out in his definition here:

> This "taxation" poses a significant dilemma for ethnic scholars because we frequently find ourselves having to respond to situations that are imposed on us by the administration, which assumes that we are best suited for specific tasks because of our race/ethnicity or our presumed knowledge of cultural differences. This taxation takes many forms, with some being easier to identify than others. A few easily identifiable forms are as follows: (a) being called upon to be the expert on matters of diversity within the organization, even though we may not be knowledgeable on the issues or very comfortable in the role; (b) being called on, often repeatedly, to educate individuals in the majority group about diversity, even though this is not part of the job description and we are not given any authority or recognition to go along with the responsibility; (c) serving on an affirmative action committee or task force that culminates in the rehashing of many of the same recommendations that we have seen in the past with little real structural change ever taking place; (d) serving as the liaison between the organization and the ethnic community, even though we may not agree with the way the organization's policies impact on the community; (e) taking time away from our own work to serve as general problem solver, troubleshooter, or negotiator for disagreements that arise in part because of sociocultural differences among the administration, staff, students, or community; and (f) being called on to translate official documents or letters to clients, or to serve as interpreters when non-English-speaking clients, visitors, or dignitaries appear at our place of employment.[12]

Reading Padilla's article was a "light bulb" moment for me—finally, someone articulated the phenomena I personally experienced and witnessed so often in higher education. The concept is enduring and interwoven into the discourse of our work and art: as when two of my heroes in the field of higher education, Professors Shaun Harper and Lori Patton Davis, recently linked the content of Beyoncé's "Break My Soul" to the uncompensated and unrecognized contributions of Black scholars, and particularly, Black women, in academia.[13]

Advancing the Struggle: Key Scholars Interpreting Cultural Taxation

Ever since reading Padilla's article, I've encouraged colleagues to read his work, as well as Dr. Geneva Gay's, who termed the form of marginality that graduate students of color encountered doing this same work as *problematic popularity*.[14] Around the same time, one of my heroes in the field, Dr. Christine Stanley, published "Coloring the Academic Landscape: Faculty of Color Breaking the Silence in Predominantly White Colleges and Universities."[15] I had long followed Dr. Stanley's research, and had even had the opportunity to engage with her as she conceptualized a manuscript when I was an editor at the *Harvard Educational Review*. I admired Dr. Stanley and considered her a role model and mentor. This impactful article brought together the work of other scholars I admired, like Drs. Caroline Sotello Viernes Turner, Bill Banks, Joe Feagin, and Linda Tillman.

Stanley's focus on the stresses upon the shoulders of Black women faculty resonated strongly with me, particularly as she presented narratives on teaching, mentoring, collegiality, and the challenge of persisting and resisting while cognizant of their identities as underrepresented and marginalized scholars in the academy. Meanwhile, the faculty in the article described how they navigated service obligations and the omnipresent specter of racism in their careers. Stanley's article chronicled the agonizing shortcomings of PWIs for underrepresented faculty, yet also issued forth a way forward to improve their status—by listening. I saw Dr. Stanley challenging me to dedicate a substantial part of my scholarly work to interpreting these stories: "For many faculty of color, who reside throughout the academic landscape, their silenced state is a burdensome cycle that is rarely broken. Only rarely are they asked to speak candidly about their experiences so that we can learn how to develop effective recruitment and retention strategies for diversifying higher education faculties."[16]

In more recent years, Drs. Tiffany Joseph and Laura Hirshfield titled their 2011 analysis of the impact of cultural taxation on the sense of belonging and career advancement for minoritized faculty, "'Why Don't You Get Somebody New to Do It?'"[17] These scholars were directing the academic community to understand the burdens carried by faculty of color, and I was mindful of this dimension in my own research. When I reflect on my scholarship, I have been particularly focused on the psychosocial impact of additional mentoring and service on marginalized faculty, typified in the story of a Black professor in a study we conducted years ago:

> Alex, a tenured professor, detailed how he invested considerable time assisting a student from another academic unit and the inordinate effort he devoted to this work: "I spent the better part of a month helping her find grants . . . I think that kept her here." The conversation illuminated how faculty found themselves "serv[ing] as general problem solver, troubleshooter, or negotiator" for disagreements among colleagues and/or students due to sociocultural differences, all despite little or no recognition in academic reward structures, including promotion and tenure, for this work. As Alex remarked, "I contemplated going to the [student's] chair and saying, 'What the hell are you doing? Why is she coming to me for money? She should be coming to you.' But where would that get me?"[18]

So many similar accounts—helping students experiencing domestic violence find support, seeking funding opportunities for students, and helping students, staff, and faculty find what bell hooks termed "homeplaces" in both the PWI and greater, overwhelmingly White, community context—illustrate what cultural taxation looks like for so many faculty, staff, and students.[19] I was subsequently asked to speak on the impact of cultural taxation in several contexts—usually after a discussion where I used the term and the other person asked, "What's cultural taxation?"

Bringing the Discourse on Cultural Taxation to a Broader Audience

Dr. Kevin Foster, a colleague and scholar-activist whose work I'd followed for years, invited me to participate in the sixth season of his Emmy-nominated PBS show, *Blackademics*. I used the opportunity to share my experience of being mentored by Dr. Charles Willie, and to challenge the idea that the exemplary support I'd received should be viewed as beyond the scope of faculty lives. The issue was, Dr. Willie and others who had supported me should not have had to make a calculation about whether they could afford to mentor my peers and me—they should have been recognized, integrated, and rewarded as developing a new generation of scholars.[20]

The PBS appearance led to other engagements, including an unexpected call from Virginia Gewin, who was writing for *Nature*. She had found my work and wanted to learn more about the taxation experienced by faculty of color. When I used the term cultural taxation, Virginia was intrigued, and we spent the next hour discussing the nuances of how faculty attempt to meet the demands of mentoring, service, and additional labor. Her June 2020 article brokered a transnational discussion via social media among scholars in the US, UK, and Canada about the institutional expectations and demands upon BIPOC, and in the UK, about Black, Asian, and minority ethnic (BAME) scholars and staff.[21]

Dr. Ahna Skop wrote, "If you're in #HigherEducation and/or in #STEM—I encourage everyone to read this article and actively listen to how each story provides actionable items so that academia and science can become a place where everyone can thrive and innovate."[22] Geologist Dr. Stephanie Suarez commented, "I am disturbed how many times I had to describe what free labor was to academics last month. And the fact that it was completely new to their vocabulary. At least in my case they were open to understanding. Here is an article that goes more in depth."[23] Neuroscientist Dr. Ubadah Sabbagh wrote, "Read this thread & internalize it as you plan your academic department's initiatives to combat systemic racism. This effort cost further contributes to inequitable experience of Black & URM scholars."[24] One of the most active social justice-focused scholars I follow, Dr. Chanda Prescod-Weinstein, started a thread filled with excellent points, such as:

- I spent 6 hours this week advising Black students. None of them from UNH. Don't want the students to feel bad about this but [people] need to know how much time some of us are putting in, weekly, because their local people won't put any time in/aren't competent.
- I am not the community mule. If you invite me to give a science talk at your school, I am not obligated to do service to your school on top of that. And this isn't about whether you pay me.
- I spent more than 6 hours this week advising white faculty—for free—on Black academic/student issues. I love my friends but y'all are getting a lot of free support from me and will ride off into the sunset with the winnings, while I'm left trying to get tenure.[25]

The *Nature* article provided a springboard for many of us to share our experiences of overwhelmedness and point out the inequities visited upon our scholarly community, akin to a collective venting across continents. Although the focus was on STEM-focused faculty, many additional tweets contributed perspectives from other areas of inquiry—and expanded the discussion to include staff members and students.

ADDRESSING CULTURAL TAXATION: WHAT CAN WE DO ABOUT IT?

Like Dr. Prescod-Weinstein, I've spent hours talking to faculty and administrators about what should be done to support emerging underrepresented scholars. I first advise them to familiarize themselves with the work of scholars such as Drs. KerryAnn O'Meara, Audrey Jaeger, Joya Misra, Courtney Lennartz, and Alexandra Kuvaeva, who have conducted studies on faculty workloads and proffer recommendations to ensure that women and BIPOC scholars are not left to take on disproportionate amounts of service. This work is also designed to address the *structural* nature of cultural taxation by getting at the roots of the inequity, which we'll discuss in depth in chapter 4.[26]

On the individual level, I also reference the work of Dr. Debra Meyerson, whose concept of *tempered radicalism* gives us the term "verbal jujitsu"—using rhetoric to respond effectively to demands on one's time.[27] The cardinal rule is to *never respond immediately to requests on your time*. It's perfectly appropriate to take a day—if not more—to consider the request before committing or turning it down. I call this flipping the script, and the following phrases both invoke how requests are taxing on individuals and place the onus on the asker to consider how they can support the underrepresented individual's trajectory and ascent in the academic sphere:

- "I'd love to do this, but my plate is full. What can you take off?"
- "I need to talk to my supervisor/mentor about taking on additional responsibilities."
- "I'm already serving in several roles. Perhaps [colleague] would be a good choice."
- "I can serve, but under these terms (time, output, etc.)."
- "How is this reflected in my academic progress?"
- "How representative is this committee of people from [identity group]? I'm concerned about being tokenized."

Note that the second bullet directly invokes mentors and supervisors. This speaks to what Charles Willie termed the intercessory function of mentors, which is when mentors "step in front" of their protégés to protect or deflect potential danger.[28] Mentors have stature in the institutional context and can usually "afford" the consequences of turning down a request—certainly, more so than the mentee. Furthermore, this approach also allows a more pragmatic engagement: the mentor might be able to negotiate more favorable terms that move a questionable request to one that provides greater rewards than the initial query.

You Can't "Just Say No" Your Way Out of It

At times, mentors and administrative leaders who are familiar with cultural taxation conclude that the best approach is to form an impenetrable wall around their mentee(s). I call this the "Nancy Reagan" approach—"just say no." While typically rooted in good intentions, this approach can deny agency to the mentee. This approach can also ignore the challenge at the core of cultural taxation: many times, the additional labor addresses concerns that are important to the underrepresented faculty, staff, or student. The committed mentor recognizes this and thinks about the cost-benefit analysis in its entirety instead of having a blanket policy.

In my own experience, I remember meeting with my advisor, Dr. Bridget Terry Long, about cochairing the Alumni of Color Conference at the Harvard GSE. As I was a cofounder of the conference, my peers were looking for me to serve as a chair along with Zenub Kakli and Shannon Hodge, emerging leaders who would serve as institutional memory keepers after I'd graduated. I was certain Bridget would tell me to prioritize my academic progress, but she surprised me when she gave her full support: "I know that this is important to you, and you need to contribute to the conference." Bridget did make it clear, however, that I would likely need to make this one of my only commitments of time and leadership at this stage of my studies.

In our research, we saw similar calculations by faculty who balanced the potential burden with a sense of community responsibility. One of our participants, "Yvonne," told us why she took on so much leadership in the campus community: "I feel like [Black faculty are] pretty privileged, and that we have a responsibility if we come from marginalized communities. It's only because of the marginalized communities that we're here."[29]

This is a sentiment I am particularly aware of as a scholar teaching in both the community and university context where I was nurtured. It's a unique circumstance to be asked to contribute and support causes that were pivotal in your own development, and it's an incredibly validating experience to address leaders in spaces that you once occupied. Dr. Victor Sáenz and I have discussed this in our scholarly personal narratives in "Coming Home: *Hermanos Académicos* Reflect on Paths and Present Realities at Their Home Institution."[30] We are proximal to the institutions that shaped us as young men at our alma mater, but at even earlier periods of our lives. (At an early faculty meeting, I noted that among my new colleagues were Dr. Bonnie Hamill, who I'd interviewed as a high school senior about educational reform, and Dr. Glenn Nolly, who was principal at Reagan High School just after I'd left there.) Due to these deep community connections, an opportunity to speak at a college preparatory organization at my alma mater, for example, is something I feel very strongly compelled to do.

Community Obligations and Responsibilities: A Tax We're Willing to Pay

This variant of service demands a different response. Having the sensitivity and taking the time to explain why some obligations aren't possible, or negotiating a way to support the mission and objectives (suggesting a colleague who can speak on an issue, or agreeing to speak at one event rather than making a semester-long commitment), is critical. For those of us raised in communities of color, the danger of being perceived as someone who is aloof or distant from the community is a real concern—and one of the most hurtful things we might experience.[31] Our connections and commitment to our home communities are often what propelled us in our careers, and those relationships require special care. I have been fortunate in my scholarly and administrative pursuits to have been enthusiastically supported in my community-facing engagements, but it's important that managers, department chairs, deans, and other leaders understand that intentional community-based work is often the most rewarding (and value-congruent) aspect of our careers. Recognition of this fact—and recognition in the form of awards, commendations, and feedback from the community—is an important aspect of supporting scholars and administrators.

An often-overlooked aspect of these community-centered engagements is that those of us from historically marginalized identity groups serve as ambassadors for our institutions, frequently building (and repairing) relationships in communities where the institutional presence has been at best, absent, or at worst, subtractive and damaging.[32] When I teach my history of higher education course, I remind my students that "town-gown" tensions are as old as universities themselves—the St Scholastica Day Riot of 1355 is a legendary example of violence and death occurring between university students and townspeople, and the founders of the University of Cambridge were Oxford scholars who fled after students were lynched there in the early thirteenth century.[33]

Repairers of the Breach: Historically Underrepresented Scholars/Practitioners and Their Brokering Between Institutions and Communities

In our modern era, the wounds inflicted by universities include economic and fiscal exploitation of surrounding communities; environmental and physical damage created by university industry and infrastructure; and the theft, exploitation, and gentrification of land, both where the institution resides and proximal to the campus. Many of these incidents and occurrences predate our presence on campus; but they often continue, invisible to many on campus but well known and resented in their adjacent communities.[34] One of the most valuable lessons I have learned is that venturing into community spaces as a listener and a learner—rather than the typical posture we assume as experts—is an excellent way to delve into the history of our institutions. And frequently, it's the less than laudatory actions of our institutions that we learn in the process. Simultaneously, we are weaving fragile threads into a trusting relationship.

Eventually, we can use our position to influence and advocate for acknowledgment and apologies for the damage done—and even engage in efforts to compensate those harmed or deprived as a result of our institution's oppressive practices. This is an exhaustive and complex undertaking, and probably more than one individual should endure. However, it's important to speak to the realities of many college and university members' engagement. These fragile initial relationships are often the ones that lead to more sustainable and systematic approaches.

As an early career teacher, I was once advised that every interaction I had with a parent or student was always within the context of their previous interactions with our school, the district, and the mechanism of education altogether. We had to be cognizant that their distrust and suspicion wasn't necessary directed at us personally, but rather at a system that had not always regarded historically underrepresented people as equal. I find the same to be true of institutions of higher education. Some in our community have benefited from an institutional affiliation, while some have been marginalized. While the de jure barriers may be eliminated, the memories and structural impediments still exist.

I can relate to this on a very personal level. In the late 1980s, I was advised by a number of older African American people to not attend The University of Texas at Austin, in part because they remembered when the university fought all the way to the Supreme Court to keep African Americans out. Indeed, Thomas Russell's 2010 article detailing the institution's efforts to circumvent the *Sweatt* decision by creating an exclusionary testing program takes its title from the words in a memo written by an administrator in 1955: "Keep Negroes Out of Most Classes Where There Are a Large Number of Girls."[35] The legacy of this position had far-reaching implications: when I was asked to take on a special project in 1996 calling African American students after the *Hopwood* decision (in which the Fifth

Circuit Court prohibited UT Austin's use of affirmative action in admissions), many students mistakenly (but given history, perhaps understandably) assumed that UT was once again employing a tactic to keep Blacks out of the university.[36]

Similarly, during the *Fisher* cases, it was important to convey that for the third time in 2014, UT was defending its use of affirmative action. The author and researcher Gary Lavergne, who wrote a brilliant biography of Heman Marion Sweatt, the African American plaintiff who won the lawsuit for the desegregation of UT Austin, related to me the amazement and humility of sitting in the Supreme Court hearing oral arguments—as a guest of the family of Heman Sweatt. Our institutional history is always actively influencing the present.

RIP IT OUT AT THE ROOT: ELIMINATING CULTURAL TAXATION . . . ?

Given all that we know about cultural taxation—what it is, examples of it, and how it can eat away at the time, treasure, and will of those most impacted by it—how do we eradicate it? Absent a sustained and committed critical cultural discourse in our social and political worlds, I actually don't think it's possible. I do, however, think it's possible to imagine a world in which cultural taxation is named, significantly reduced, and rewarded and recognized. As I've mentioned previously, many of the scholars and administrators I've interviewed over the years have discussed how they are willing to pay a cultural tax—it is an obligation and commitment that moors them in their positions.

> Yvonne, tenured, stated, "It is a wage. It is a tax. You can feel angry about it, but without it, I don't think I would want to be here." Throughout the interview, Yvonne discussed how working with students and colleagues on professional, academic, and social issues left her feeling not only drained but also needed in the community.

> Similarly, Nathan, untenured, saw himself as a repository of knowledge about academia. He stated, "Those are the things that I'll pass on, and so, it's also sociocultural capital."[37]

Another tenured scholar in this study, David, eloquently discussed how the existence of cultural taxation suggested that there was in fact a community that both demanded and supported his presence: "I think [cultural taxation] is absolutely the case, but I wouldn't have it any other way. To feel responsible to the community, it means there is a community to feel responsible to . . . because there is some kind of expectation and reciprocity one way or the other."[38]

Considering the Mental (and Physical) Health Toll

At the same time, there is a growing recognition that racism is a public health crisis across the US. According to a 2021 analysis by Salud America!, a national Latino-focused organization centered at UT Health San Antonio, 111 city councils, 78 county boards, 16 mayors, 4 state governors, 5 state legislatures, 7 universities, 4 school boards, and 16 nonprofit organizations have made resolutions or declarations to this effect.[39] Such proclamations have their origins in research by scholars such as Dr. Sherman James, who in 1983 observed the phenomena he labeled "John Henryism" among working-class Black men, which we'll discuss in greater depth in chapter 6. I revisited James's pioneering work soon after the murder of George Floyd, in an opinion piece in *Fortune*. It was at a protest, which I attended with my children, that I realized that we were all at our breaking point:

> During a march last week, a colleague talked about all the spaces they were a part of: community organizations, social justice collectives, professional obligations, and work. I looked around at my fellow Black faculty and administrators and realized we were all doing the same high-impact, but also high-emotional-toll, types of activities.

> But at the same time, we were attempting to keep all the plates spinning in our chaotic professional lives in a manner that exceeded that of our nonblack peers.[40]

John Henry, for those unfamiliar, is a fictional steel driver in a folk tale who races a drilling machine to bore out a tunnel. He defeats the machine only to immediately suffer a heart attack from overwork. I remember John Henry from elementary school folk tale lessons because he was the only Black folk hero I can recall, but I also felt the bittersweet recognition that he dies in the end.

My own realization that John(etta) Henryism existed in my profession was at one of the most centering scholarly convenings I have ever participated in, the Career Enhancement Fellowship Retreat held by the Institute for Citizens and Scholars (formerly known as the Woodrow Wilson National Fellowship Foundation). I was in my third year on the tenure track and still feeling that I had somehow lucked into the professoriate, still a "guest in someone else's house" (a quote from Ron Wakabayashi of the Japanese American Citizens League, and the title of a groundbreaking 1994 article from my hero Dr. Caroline Sotello Viernes Turner). Then one of the mentors at the conference, Dr. Donna M. Weir-Soley, shared reflections on her career. Donna struck me as one of the most grounded and "real" people I'd met in academia, because we bonded over our shared Jamaican heritage, food, and raising kids—no discussion over our accolades and professional accomplishments. But what Donna shared chilled me to the bone. She recounted the stories of her mentors, virtually all women of color, and virtually all dead at an early age. Recently, my *Black Austin Matters* cohost, colleague, and friend Dr. Lisa B. Thompson related a similar story about Black women she admired in the academy. If academia was supposed to be a privileged place, it now began to appear to be a dangerous place.

Years later, I would read the harrowing story of Dr. Thea Hunter, an adjunct professor at many institutions including the City College of

New York, whose excessive workload—and lack of health insurance—led to her death from multi-organ failure. As Adam Harris's *Atlantic* article stated, Dr. Hunter became "trapped in academia's permanent underclass," exploited by a system that is constantly consuming. Harris aptly notes, "Academia is not an easy road for anyone to take, but especially not for women of color, and especially not for those who have been consigned to the adjunct underclass."[41] I reflected on this tragedy when my friend and mentor Dr. James Wilson, who was serving as associate provost at Prairie View A&M University and was one of my greatest champions, died far too young in June 2020. I share these stories as a testament to the lives these scholars led, and a reminder that none of us are promised tomorrow. We deserve careers and workplaces that enrich and sustain us, and we must endeavor to keep the health and well-being of our citizens at the forefront. This is even more true as we struggle through a pandemic and endure intense racial and economic crises. Sadly, and perhaps predictably, those of us from underrepresented communities will suffer disproportionately from the consequences of a professional, social, and politically stressful period.

WORK-LIFE BALANCE, THE ACADEMIC RACHET, AND A PANDEMIC

I've been accused of being a "me-searcher"—and I have no problem admitting this, as one of the reasons I have researched the topics that intrigue me is because there simply aren't many chronicles of experiences such as mine. This is what inspired my colleague Dr. Aaron Rochlen and me to research the experiences of academic fathers—we were able to learn a great deal from the experiences of women scholars and their navigation of careers and motherhood but found the issue of fatherhood and academic careers fairly unexamined. Since our research with Joe Grasso, Erin Reilly, and Daniel Spikes, I have thought more about how work-life balance is given short shrift in academic careers, and how we tend to shy away from engaging in discussion about how we subordinate our health, families, and mental well-being for fear of not being successful—tenure, promotion, publishing, grants, and so forth, something we will discuss more in chapter 6. While I do think there is greater focus on work-life balance during the pandemic, my worry is that this is temporal. When the pandemic recedes, will there be a rush to "normalcy," without an analysis of how "normal" is not truthfully a sustainable career path? I think about how analytics and things like acceptance rates, h- and i-indices, and grants serve as indicators and predictors of academic success—but how hollow and lacking these indicators can be when it comes to who will support emerging scholars and engage in the significant service commitments that come with advancement in the academy.

Academic leaders need to be the strongest voices when it comes to work-life balance, and acknowledge that for all of our technological advances, days are only twenty-four hours long. I've never understood the idea that as time progresses, we tighten the academic ratchet and expect scholars to accomplish more *with the same array of time*. Raising a family, supporting elders, and being a whole person outside of work is more time consuming than ever—where do academic standards acknowledge these realities? At the core of this, to me, is an inherent distrust of scholarly activity and how it looks different from discipline to discipline and person to person. This is further complicated by the fact that some of the most innovative and exciting work that scholars and administrators do is collaborative work, which by its nature is complex, destabilizing, and time consuming. As a serial collaborator, I've come to realize that what has been the most sustaining work I have done as a scholar is the most dangerous, as the outcomes are not guaranteed to bear academic fruit (high teaching evaluations, articles, grants, etc.).

Resisting the Pace: Tempered Radicalism in the Classroom

When I think about being subversive in my academic career, my teaching collaboration with my colleagues Dr. Julia Mickenberg (a historian) and

Kate Catterall (a designer) was probably one of the pinnacles of rebellion. We met in a provost-led de-siloing initiative and soon found ourselves gravitating toward an idea of a combined course, with students from different disciplines, levels, and pedagogical approaches. Unsurprisingly, the first (and only) draft was not as successful as we had hoped, especially using the traditional methods of evaluation, like course evaluations. But we felt the importance of examining the raw, and at times painful, reflection of the pedagogical experience and discovered many points of pride and success—or promising starts, at the very least. We collectively stated:

> Our recommendation for those seeking to de-silo their academic lives is to think about how the process itself might be leveraged for the currency needed for tenure, promotion, and recognition, even as we'd confirm that the best reason to collaboratively teach across disciplines is that it makes us grow as thinkers, teachers, scholars, and people. It is a sad reality that the push for greater faculty productivity leads us to consider our teaching in relation to quantifiable metrics of "productivity." [C]ollaboration and de-siloing the academy in the current political climate in our state and nation is a risky proposition.[42]

Our work met many of the characteristics that Meyerson posits for tempered radicals. Our individual efforts found synergy in our collaboration, which also brought in scholars and administrators across our campus and well beyond. One course was a seemingly small effort, but every guest we brought to the classroom left buzzing with ideas about how we, and they, could leverage the shared learning in other contexts. Many conversations emerged from the class, initially from the faculty and administrators we invited, but later from the students themselves. We sought powerful friends rather than taking on a deeply entrenched system: the special advisor to the provost and the deputy to the president for strategy and policy helped us with financial resources and a stamp of approval.

We certainly didn't expect revolutionary change, but we demonstrated that time, commitment, and patience could slowly present opportunities for our field to reconsider teaching, collaborating, and application to real world problems—while managing to remain friends throughout the process. Years later, we can see more opportunities and endorsements for cross-disciplinary endeavors at our university, so perhaps our collaboration had some influence. We did this all, however, with the protection of tenure—an almost necessary shield to tinker and reassess the metrics and values considered for pedagogy, research, and as is often said at our university, "changing the world."[43]

CULTURAL TAXATION IN A PERIOD OF RACIAL RECKONING: THE DISPROPORTIONATE IMPACT ON BIPOC COMMUNITIES, PARTICULARLY BLACK WOMEN

When reflecting on the combined course and all that came with it, Julia, Kate, and I realized that we were from underrepresented identities in our disciplines, and more broadly, in the academy. A Jewish woman, Irish woman, and Black man were by no means "insiders" at a research-intensive university in the southern United States. In fact, in many ways we found each other because we were the ones who would step up (or not be diligent enough to step back) when service work was needed in our departments, colleges, and university. Regrettably, those who are culturally taxed are often in the company of others experiencing similar outcomes, and this is particularly true in the diversity, equity, inclusion, and belonging space. The impact on BIPOC populations, particularly Black women, has been profound, particularly in the past two years when a global pandemic and moment of racial reckoning have presented an unprecedented challenge for those who are most marginalized in higher education settings.

Simply put, the rarely acknowledged but essential aspects of life—pregnancy, childbirth, adoption, child-rearing, daycare, elder care, and care for the chronically ill—are disproportionately carried by women, and Black and BIPOC women in particular often bear an assortment of these responsibilities, sometimes alone.[44] If one layers the microaggressive, microinvalidating climate that is frequently a part of predominantly White institutions of higher education, it is easy to see how these pressures can manifest in damaged health (recall the examples earlier in this chapter) or a desire and decision to leave the environment altogether.

The Gallup Center on Black Voices found that one in four Black and Hispanic workers reported recent discrimination at work, with the reporting being highest among young Black employees.[45] Remote work, made a necessity during the pandemic, showed BIPOC professionals a new way of working with reduced microaggressions and code-switching. It should be no surprise that many have sought employment opportunities that allow flexible work arrangements. (One hidden aspect of pandemic living is that Black people, particularly women, are constantly dealing with unwanted attention to their hair in the workplace, so hair maintenance is a priority. With salons and barbershops closed, yet another barrier to their participation came into view. As my own barber Joe Harper Jr. shared in a podcast episode, "Barbers and stylists are essential workers for Black folks."[46])

STRUCTURAL CHANGE: HOW PROMOTION, TENURE, AND OTHER PROCESSES NEED TO ATTEND TO CULTURAL TAXATION

When I give talks about cultural taxation, there are usually two guaranteed reactions: knowing nods from BIPOC, queer, and women folks who are quite familiar with the examples and can contribute many of their own, and surprise and shock from organizational leaders. Fortunately, I am often asked: "What should we be doing to make sure that nobody is taking on additional labor without compensation or recognition?"

The answer is in the question. Compensation and recognition can go a long way in rectifying the imbalance. Compensation is often financial, but it doesn't have to be. Having cultural taxation work considered as part of one's work week rather than as "volunteer" work is one way of doing this. Added flexibility in one's work arrangement can help as well—as well as tracking one's work on DEI initiatives, much like how lawyers tabulate billable hours. If a manager or department chair receives a significant bill, a discussion about why one person is enduring so much should be in order.

Recognition—having public acknowledgment of one's contributions—is another investment that pays off significantly. Cultural taxation is often synonymous with invisible labor, so the simple act of sharing with colleagues that one person's mentoring of BIPOC students has led to an increase in student retention, or another person's holding of a forum for underrepresented members of the community has contributed to a sense of belonging and safety can go far in validating these efforts.[47] The work is appreciated, not taken for granted, and shown to be a value-added item to people in the institution. To go one step further, awards that can be added to a résumé or vita further signal how students, faculty, and staff are contributing to community and enhancing our educational mission. (If these awards come with remuneration, ever better!)

What Heads, Chairs, and Mentors Should Do

While these factors are important for those who are seeking advancement in the academic realm, purposive mentoring is equally important. A program head or department chair should regularly meet with early career faculty, assessing how much service they are taking on, and ensure that the service loads are evenly distributed throughout the program or department. Instead of dissuading faculty from taking on service, a better tactic is to ask the faculty member what their goals are in their community-based work and then strategize about how they can maximize their impact. For example, serving on a community nonprofit board might be a way to leverage expertise and experience while providing prestige and status to the work the faculty member is doing. Boards tend to meet regularly and predictably as well.

An additional strategy is to think of ways to create scholarly currency in one's cultural taxation work—a cultural tax shelter, if you will. Writing an op-ed about one's work mentoring or service and/or bringing attention to a lack of resources in a community is not only helpful to those whom one is serving, but it is also something that can be added to a vita. Depending on the field, there are also opportunities to write articles about the service one commits to in journals, book chapters, and handbooks. (This is where having a broad constellation of mentors across disciplines helps—there are scholarly outlets interested in articles such as these.)

I once advised a new faculty member, "For every five hours you contribute service, there should be a line on your CV denoting that." My caveat is that those lines should not only be in the "service" section of your vita. If you find yourself mentoring several students weekly, ask to have that arrangement structured as a course. (Depending on the institutional rules, it could be a recognized course in the catalog or an informal one, but it can be listed on your vita as teaching.) A long-term relationship with a community organization might provide you with enough data to create an article on the organization's history, importance, and impact. And while there are scholarly venues for publications, publishing in journalistic venues is an option too—just be sure to get advice from those in your field about what "counts."

Leaders should also be willing to step into the intercessory role for early career faculty. Some department chairs inform their faculty that they must clear any service roles with their chair first—not out of a need to control, but to provide an "out" for junior faculty. The faculty member can then review the "ask" with their chair and get advice regarding whether they should accept the obligation or deny it. If the decision is made that the "ask" is not worthwhile, the faculty member can simply say that their chair denied the role. Additionally, if the work is necessary and important, the chair can reallocate assignments on departmental committees—for instance, if a faculty member is spending considerable time traveling to recruit underrepresented students, that faculty member can be removed from another committee assignment (with the caveat that it is better to give up a high-workload, modest-prestige committee than the opposite).

At the time when a scholar is making the case for their promotion, there are things that the candidate can do, and things that those of us who serve as external reviewers can do. For candidates, cultural taxation work should be woven into your research and teaching narratives—not just your service statement. Perhaps you mentor first generation students in your lab, because you recognize that they may not have had the same opportunities in high school as other students. Or you mentor students who have taken your class beyond the semester, extending their learning on the topic beyond the course. The cohesion and connection of your academic legacy is not bound to just one part of your dossier.

For external referees, I always emphasize how the candidate's leadership in the community informs their research. A scholar who serves on the DEI committee for their scholarly society is not only doing a nice thing, but is also shaping the society—and the field/subfield's commitment to scholarship across diverse populations. A scholar who writes op-eds in local newspapers is serving the public interest (something that a state flagship such as UT Austin is supposed to do). In other words, speak to the candidate's research contributions and capabilities—but also connect them to their cultural taxation.

Ultimately, for those of us who sit on advisory committees that wield decision-making power over promotion and tenure candidates, we must start using terms such as "cultural taxation" to refute concerns about scholarly productivity, if the evidence is there. Closely reviewing vitas and noticing who is on recruitment committees, who serves as the minority liaison in departments, and such, can point to a structural issue where a faculty member from a particular identity group is being asked to serve in ways that others are not (indeed, there is a term for that—*privilege payoff*—that we will discuss in the next chapter).

This critical role of senior scholars—to stand up and call out inequities—came vividly to life as I sat on a panel of colleagues on mentoring.

Unsurprisingly, we all were BIPOC, and all except me were women. We had a robust discussion, with many of the best exchanges coming from our *other* women colleagues in the room who were mentoring junior colleagues. One of the final comments came from a male colleague, who essentially decried the heavy emphasis on scholarly metrics but in essence shrugged his shoulders, saying, "But what can we do?"

"What we *must* do," I responded, "is go to our scholarly societies and form task forces that name the invisible labor that women and BIPOC scholars do, ensure that our external review letters speak to the service and cultural taxation that candidates perform and how it makes them *better* scholars and colleagues, and finally, do what you're doing. Commit to a mentoring practice that is prestigious and rewards you and your mentee for your selection, and serve as a coprincipal investigator or coauthor so your mentee can accrue the benefits we take for granted as a function of our own privilege and stature in our respective fields."

I wasn't intending to write a final paragraph of a chapter about balancing DEI work with the need to make sure we're all pulling our weight, but that's essentially what happened.

CHAPTER FOUR

Addressing the Privilege Payoff

Ensuring That All Hands Are on Deck with DEI

NOW THAT WE HAVE A COMMON definition and realization that cultural taxation exists, let's turn our focus to the converse perspective—how those who hold privileged identities in academic institutions are provided more time, fewer interruptions, and fewer service commitments, therefore providing an advantage as they too strive for the same rewards of promotion, tenure, and merit. I have termed this benefit the "privilege payoff." In this chapter, I will first describe the phenomenon. While I am certain that there are those who intentionally shirk DEI responsibilities and allow their colleagues to take on this work, I argue that, like many forms of advantage, the privilege payoff operates invisibly in the background. Therefore, one aspect of this chapter will be to provide awareness of how the majority of faculty and staff benefit from nonobligatory commitments to DEI work.

Next, we will examine how social loafing and other noncollegial behaviors in academic departments and units can exacerbate cultural taxation and increase the burden of academic housekeeping, particularly impacting minoritized members of the community. The work on equitable service workloads informs this chapter, with best practices to enable department and unit leaders to assess and respond to inequities in service, particularly those surrounding diversity and inclusion work. As a closing to this chapter, I will invoke the importance of higher education leaders listening to and following the scholarship of minoritized researchers, who have advanced these concerns in both peer-reviewed venues and public scholarship, leaning into the concept of cultural humility—the "self-reflective examination of one's own culture" that "can serve as a launching point for learning about other cultures—and can be an asset in understanding how assumptions and biases shape one's world view."[1] This further emphasizes that all members of the campus community have a role to play in engaging with and celebrating inclusion, rather than it being an issue to be "managed" by specialists in the area—awarded this status by virtue of their identity.

YES, CULTURAL TAXATION IS A "THING"

Introducing leaders in higher education to Padilla's concept of cultural taxation, or the Black/Brown/pink/queer tax, has been alternately positive and frustrating.[2] The positive aspect is that it brings awareness to the climatic concerns experienced by historically marginalized populations. The frustrating side, however, is that it leaves me wondering: How is it that a phenomenon so familiar and known to underrepresented people in higher education can be so veiled or unknown to our more advantaged colleagues? In my mind, it's a clear manifestation of how systems of privilege work, as Peggy McIntosh articulates: "As a white person, I realized I had been taught about racism as something which puts others at a disadvantage, but had been taught not to see one of its corollary aspects, white privilege, which puts me at an advantage."[3]

Systems of privilege purposefully veil advantages, rendering them invisible, so that only a very thorough self-reflection and analysis brings them forth. As anti-racist educator Dr. Bob Jensen has said to me, "Once you understand privilege exists, and you are a beneficiary, you have to act."[4] Certainly, that action can be inaction—simply allowing systems to filter and advantage some while continuing to diminish and oppress others. Or it can be performative—guilt, lamentation, and anger—but lead to no meaningful change. Or it can be aimed at disassembling structures of inequity in the personal, professional, and cultural realms; work that is both small and significant. The actions I describe at the end of chapter 3 fit this category.

BLAMING THE VICTIM: MOVING FROM DEFICIT FRAMINGS OF THE CULTURALLY TAXED

A further concern when discussing cultural taxation is the gaze on marginalized people. I have noticed how quickly empathy and interest can slide into deficit framings of those impacted by cultural taxation. Without a systematic analysis, it's easy to start thinking that those who are culturally taxed are "missing something": Are they lacking in assertiveness? Localizing the problem within those who are most affected, again, allows the inequitable perpetual motion machine to persist . . . "Pay no attention to the man behind the curtain!" I found myself detailing cultural taxation while simultaneously defending the people impacted by it, all at once.

Around the same time, I read an article in *Salon* by political commentator Chauncey DeVega that discussed a study by social science researchers Willer and Wetts that found that White Americans were willing to cut social welfare programs that benefited them if they believed that similar benefits would extend to Black and other BIPOC Americans.[5] In DeVega's analysis, he notes that federal programs, such as FHA home programs and the GI Bill, provided wealth creation and intergenerational wealth transfer, and the emergence of a predominantly White middle class.[6] The casting of Black women as "welfare queens" during Ronald Reagan's 1976 presidential campaign stands in stark contrast to the fact that the biggest beneficiaries of federal poverty reduction programs are working-class Whites without college degrees.[7] DeVega's larger point is that the welfare state is defined by those who are most vilified, people of color and immigrants, while the same programs, and what Dr. Suzanne Mettler terms the "submerged state"—capital gains, tax credits and cuts, and mortgage interest deductions—operate invisibly, beyond scrutiny, silently advantaging their beneficiaries.[8] These privileges are framed as rewards for hard work rather than plainly acknowledged as a redistribution of resources to advantage those who have access.

I applied this framing to my own study of workloads and service in academia. There was also a "submerged state" of advantages—reduced advising loads, releases and reduction in committee work, and a general absence of mandated diversity, equity, and inclusion work—for the privileged groups in academia; primarily, but not exclusively, the White, upper-middle-class, cisgender, male, temporarily abled bodied, native-English-speaking faculty, staff, and administrators. Why, I wondered, were we not looking at this population equally closely?

Of course, a number of scholars in my circle were examining this. Since 2017, I've had the pleasure of working with a community of scholars who study issues related to faculty careers. Under the leadership of Dr. Vicki Baker, Drs. Jaime Lester, Aimee Terosky, and I have held midcareer faculty workshops at the annual meetings for both the Association for the Study of Higher Education (ASHE) and the American Educational Research Association (AERA)—with the memory of the late Dr. Kelly Ward, who was a part of our sessions before her passing.[9] As folks who personally experienced cultural taxation, we advised caution to our faculty participants and provided strategies on how to mitigate cultural taxation. We needed to trouble the waters regarding how many of our participants felt that the burdens of service to underrepresented populations rested on their shoulders alone.

TOWARD A THEORY OF THE PRIVILEGE PAYOFF

Inspired, I started to put the ideas on paper. If there was a community being levied a tax, there was a larger community "sheltered" from paying this tax—they were in fact receiving a "tax cut:" "[I]f cultural taxation exists, then so must a 'privilege payoff.' If minorities carry an invisible burden, those who hold dominant identities in the academy, exempted from such diversity work, find themselves getting ahead."[10] As I wrote, I recalled experiences from graduate school where I had witnessed our faculty of color "rock stars" and the legions of students seeking them out for office hours, career guidance, and mentoring—in contrast to their colleagues who had modest, or nonexistent lines of students demanding their time.

Over time, I became that professor, advising and mentoring both students in my courses and those who had been referred by their peers. My own research conveyed narratives from Black faculty of their mentoring "out of position"—a student in need of financial and emotional support would find a sympathetic Black faculty member, who then would expend the energy and effort to support the student. Often, the work was invisible and difficult to have acknowledged—our academic silos would challenge the concept of applying effort to support students from a different program, department, or school. When the faculty member would ask, "Have you asked your advisor or someone in your program to help?" often the student would reply:

> "My advisor said they can't help me with my concerns."
> "My advisor makes me feel worse after going to them. In fact, I avoid them."
> "My advisor tries to help, but they're disconnected from any power structures that can actually change things."

Faculty with privileged identities allied with underrepresented communities do notice these inequities, but often opt out of ways of helping. For instance, the concern about being a nonhomophilous mentor may arise (something I address in chapter 2). Another concern centers around fears of intimacy—for someone who has had a life buttressed by privilege, there is a sense of shame about having access to resources that a potential advisee or mentee may not have had.

Carrots and Sticks: Why Some Faculty and Staff Avoid Service Responsibilities

One of the most pernicious issues relates to how academia rewards (and ignores or punishes) some activities in relation to others. At a research-intensive institution, extramural funding and research productivity are greatly rewarded (and in contrast, deficiencies in these realms are punished). One does not have to be a cynic to realize that investing effort in seeking grants and publishing has a much higher upside than advising, mentoring, and otherwise committing to service activities—given that each of us only has twenty-four hours in each day. It's also easy to rationalize investing effort in the rewarding activities while imagining that the developmental work is being done by professional track and adjunct faculty or the student affairs specialists on campus.

This tends to be a gendered and raced divide, something we came to realize in our work on radical pedagogy and experimentation in the academy, and that Guarino and Borden have termed "academic housekeeping."[11] For BIPOC and other minoritized people in academia, there is a discomfort in "offloading" this work to colleagues with whom we share many traits—so a sense of guilt may set in and even efforts to engage in the work at the same level as our peers who are not on the tenure track. However, for some, the rationalization works thus: "That's not my job," or "That's part of the reason why those people are not on the tenure track—they're more interested in supporting students than in research." Implicit in this thought is a pecking order that elevates research activity over all other scholarly activity.

I can recall an example of this years ago, when my department chair started a faculty meeting by displaying a chart of student advising, listing each faculty member and the number of advisees they supervised. Unsurprisingly, the distribution was not equitable—many of the senior faculty advised fewer students. Among the junior faculty, the racial and gender difference between those with heavier loads was similarly observable. What was most striking, however, was the response: mostly indifference and excuse making regarding the pursuit of research and grants (something that applies to everyone in the department). Reading a little deeper, I perceived that some of our colleagues were looking at us as if we were in a Tex Avery cartoon and would morph into suckers—"It's your own fault for taking on these students!" Clearly, if the goal was to spur discussion about the (in)visible inequities in advising, it didn't land.

Indeed, in inherently competitive spaces such as university departments, it makes some sense to some to "streamline" one's activity and avoid as many service obligations as possible. After all, service awards typically come at the senior level. Most "gaps" or "flat spots" around service on vitas at the time of tenure can be easily explained by noting that the scholar was trying to establish their research or seeking grants. There's also an undercurrent of sex-role stereotyping, where women are assumed and expected to take on nurturing and developmental roles. In an early study I conducted, I interviewed a woman scholar in a quantitative field who informed me that the assumptions I brought to the study, as someone using a critical race pedagogy conceptual framework, were mistaken, as she viewed herself as a scientist first and a woman second. However, as our discussion continued, the scientist related a story about a male student who was going through a series of life challenges midway through his graduate program: health issues and ultimately a divorce.

In a meeting reviewing student progress, this unfortunate student's name came up, and his performance in the past year was roundly criticized by the faculty—moving rapidly to a decision to dismiss the student from the program. My participating scientist shared that she was the only person who seemed to care, or consider, his personal circumstances. As she advocated for the student, a male colleague simply said, "We're not here to deal with personal problems. If you're so invested in this student, it seems that you should be the one to work with him, since you're convinced he has potential." As she related this story, I noticed her realization that despite her efforts to not be forced into the role of nurturer, it nonetheless happened. Even women who resist sex-role stereotyping can find themselves in those roles.[12]

Much of what I've discussed here relates to the organizational dynamic known as *social loafing*.[13] Simply put, this is the tendency in group settings to avoid certain tasks under the assumption that *someone else* will pick up the slack. Social loafing tends to occur in larger organizations, but a major contributor to its existence is when charting or noting service contributions is difficult or nonexistent. Fortunately, there has been scholarship devoted to describing these behaviors—and some solutions.

THE RESEARCH ON FACULTY WORKLOADS

Thinking about these experiences, I also considered the zeal that the IRS exhibits in chasing down those who evade taxes. Shouldn't there be an Eliot Ness "Untouchables" group focusing on academics and administrators who accrued advantages from not engaging in this work? Along with my colleagues Baker, Lester, Terosky, and Ward, I soon encountered the work of Dr. KerryAnn O'Meara at the University of Maryland. O'Meara's research was creating a buzz, as she and her colleagues had created tools to accurately measure faculty workloads at the departmental level toward the goal of workload equity. After talking to KerryAnn and delving into her research, I read the results of the randomized control study on work assignments and rewards in academic departments.[14] By following four steps—providing departmental workshops on implicit bias and how it relates to both the amount and type of workload assigned to women and minority faculty members; creating dashboards providing transparency on service, teaching, and research duties; using these dashboards to expose inequities; and providing professional development webinars to discuss their plans to deal with these inequities, participating departments were significantly more likely than control departments to report both conditions and practices supporting equity and a willingness to address workload equity concerns in their departments.[15] Soon after encountering this work, in my role as my college's chief diversity officer, I worked with department chairs and college leaders to chart all of our departmental and college-wide committee assignments, noting the members' race, gender, and rank, as well as the relative workload level (light, medium, heavy) and prestige (low, medium, and high) of the committees. This exhausting yet necessary activity allowed us for the first time to track who carried the weight individually, and collectively, in the essential work of leading our departments and college.

Proximal Experiences of Being Othered

In conceptualizing the privilege payoff, I drew on another concept from my research, proximal experiences of being othered, which I introduced in chapter 2. This theory emerged in my research on White faculty mentors of Black students: while Black faculty engaged in developmental relationships with Black students tended to draw on similar experiences navigating predominantly White institutions—being the only or one of a few BIPOC students in a classroom or a lab, navigating microaggressions, and the like—it wasn't as clear how White faculty engaged in their mentoring with Black students. But as I interviewed more White mentors, a pattern emerged.

Initially when I asked the question, "Why do you think you are an effective mentor to Black students?" most participants replied with confusion. They mentored students from diverse backgrounds, and they didn't necessarily see anything special about how they approached Black students. But when I countered that I had distributed a survey to Black students at the institution, and had specifically sought to interview White faculty who multiple students had identified as a mentor, they too asked themselves the same question. What emerged were stories—stories about family experiences and formative years—where these White faculty were acutely aware of their own marginal identity within Whiteness.[16]

It first came to light in talking with Jewish faculty participants—who all pointed to a cultural identity of being discriminated against, and in some instances, personal experiences of losing relatives in the Holocaust. Oppression was not an abstraction to them; they could connect to marginalization in a visceral, lived manner. I also heard stories from one professor about them spending time with their Italian grandparents who had immigrated at the turn of the century and lived in an East Coast city's "Little Italy" because they were unable to find housing and work in other parts of the city. Another professor described growing up as a German youth in Scandinavia, and being on the periphery of social groups in school because of his accent. And another professor shared how her younger brother came out in a small, conservative town—and her decision to vocally support her sibling, losing friends and becoming a subject of gossip in the community. She was unyielding in her support of her brother, which meant that she witnessed her circle of friends shrink.[17]

The marginalization experiences typically happened when they were young, and they were not episodic—rather, they were ongoing and they spent many years negotiating feelings of exclusion and periphery. They also tended to befriend other people who experienced marginalization, and similarly took on their pain empathetically. One professor's eyes welled up with tears when he related the story of visiting a favorite lunch spot—which he frequented almost daily—with a Black woman friend. While he was used to being seated immediately and receiving a high level of service, this particular day he and his friend were ignored until he told the server they were waiting to be seated. His observation of how his friend seemed resigned to this kind of treatment led him to share, "That experience . . . it infuriated me, and saddened me."[18]

Proximal experiences of being othered such as the ones I've discussed here—the times in life when majority-identity faculty have been marginalized or have experienced a diminished sense of belonging—are *potentially* experiences that can be mined for empathy and understanding. I feel the need to state this very carefully, as proximal experiences are not equivalent experiences. As painful as anti-Semitism, sexism, homophobia, and ableism, to name some of these forms of discrimination are, they are not the same, and a well-intentioned mentor may entirely miss the mark if they intimate that their oppression is identical. This should not be interpreted as "the mentee's cultural taxation is worse than mine"—it is simply different. Facile comparisons can lead to what Elizabeth "Betita" Martinez and Ange-Marie Hancock have termed "oppression Olympics"—a "futile hierarchy of suffering," as Angela Davis has stated.[19] These exercises can work against intersectional solidarity and collective equity work.

Instead, proximal experiences of being othered provide an empathetic bridge for connecting at the most visceral level over marginalizing experiences. While we can intellectualize and describe the effect of microaggressions or microinvalidations, linking to the sinking feeling in one's stomach or the sense of dread that is frequently an aspect of existing in predominantly White spaces is a level of empathy appreciated by those experiencing such stress. Proximal experiences sharpen senior colleagues' sensibility about what it might feel like to be an underrepresented person in a space that is indifferent to hostile regarding their existence. A natural evolution of this state of mind is moving to action, inspiring one to think about how to leverage their privilege on behalf of those less represented.

ENGAGING THE PRIVILEGE PAYOFF THROUGH LISTENING AND VALIDATION

Once majority faculty and administrators understand what the privilege payoff is, there are notable things they can do to halt the inequitable distribution of labor and responsibilities. Most apparent is listening to the voices of BIPOC, women, queer, differently abled, and other minoritized scholars and practitioners who can vividly convey the toll of cultural taxation on their terms. One of the most insightful anthologies is Dr. Patricia A. Matthew's *Written/Unwritten*, which brings together voices of BIPOC women, queer BIPOC women, and faculty of color, and discusses their efforts to gain footholds in the academic landscape, presenting the dilemma that BIPOC faculty engage with: "figure[ing] out how to cope with (confront, deflect, or absorb) the daily microaggressions of the academy while trying to navigate structural obstacles that everyone faces in environments that are either maddeningly indifferent or hostile."[20] There are other voices to hear, as well, and those in need of validation—likely in the institutions where we work and learn. When I present to academic leaders on cultural taxation and the privilege payoff, I urge them to spend time listening to their colleagues' experiences, explicitly asking them how they have resisted and persisted in predominantly White institutional spaces. Even those colleagues assumed to be "satisfied" will relate stories of frustration and rage that may not have had an outlet previously. Hearing these reflections and resisting the urge to challenge or deflect ("Why didn't you tell me or file a grievance?") is an important stage. The validation of these experiences allows the space for the acknowledgment of these experiences as real and damaging.

To enact structural change, there is a need to make personal change. When I talk to academic leaders about cultural taxation, I sometimes hear abrupt assessments of experiences, centering the problem on how the faculty member or administrator handled the harm, rather than alleviating and eliminating the source of the harm. And another variation is a paternalistic approach to seize control of marginalized faculty and administrators' agency and become a gatekeeper: "I'm not going to allow them to take on additional responsibilities." Thankfully, I also hear leaders' empathy when relating what they have learned from their marginalized colleagues.

Cultural Humility as a Corrective Lens to the Privilege Payoff

For those leaders, they draw on cultural humility, a concept originating with medical educators Drs. Melanie Tervalon and Jann Murray-Garcia, which in essence decenters one's own experiences and considers how other cultural identities understand and experience the world.[21] Tervalon and Murray-Garcia posit three aspects of cultural humility: first, an understanding that the self-evaluation and self-critique of cultural humility is lifelong. No matter how many workshops one attends, books one reads, or certifications one accrues, the need to remain eternally curious and eternally learning exists. There is no magical threshold that announces one's status as a culturally humble person; it is the commitment to the journey of understanding that matters. Second, the culturally humble practitioner must leverage their positionality and privilege to address power imbalances in organizational settings. Increasing awareness of these inequitable circumstances and acting to rectify them represents how one can be an advocate.[22]

An example of this emerged as I worked with a team of faculty and administrators in an inclusive faculty search committee workshop. Watching a dramatization of deliberations after a fictional search committee completed their interviews, many of the participants observed that when the older, senior, cisgender White male professor spoke, the deliberations tracked toward his preferred candidate—and the discussion of the others diminished. Strategizing on ways to allow all of the members of the group to contribute, we came up with two approaches: first, the least powerful members of the committee—the nontenured, younger members—should be the first to speak. Not only does this allow their voices to be heard, but it also acknowledges that they are likely the closest to the job candidates, in terms of experience, and can provide insightful evaluative comments. Second, the most powerful voice, represented by the older, senior, cisgender White male, can leverage his position by assuming the role of a "catalyst": he can monitor whose voices are recognized, hold process time for those more reluctant to speak by encouraging the group to take moments of silence to think and then respond, and ask questions like "How conversant was the candidate regarding issues of gender equity?" rather than leaving it to women committee members to ask the question.

The catalyst can also inform the members of the committee that he is accessible and available to all members, and can even meet with the junior members to let them know that they can raise concerns with him privately, which he can then bring to the group—so individuals from a particular identity aren't singled out as being a "special interest pleader." The catalyst also becomes more aware and alert to issues of inclusion and equity in his role—raising the questions, regardless of whether other members raise them or not. What I like about the catalyst role is that it publicly acknowledges what most people in the group observe—where the power traditionally lies—and then provides the catalyst with agency to disrupt the inequitable patterns. Rather than feeling guilt or resentment for having that social status, he is invited to "use his powers for good."

The third aspect of cultural humility centers on the power of partnership in enacting relationships for learning with communities.[23] Recognizing communities' cultural wealth, as Dr. Tara Yosso states, and envisioning partnerships with community members as essential to our ability to do our work credibly means that community engagement is ongoing and reflective.[24] Cultural humility rejects the idea of communities "lacking" and brings forth the idea that communities are critical partners in solutions. Vitally, this comes with a caveat: the culturally humble practitioner is not a passive empty vessel to be filled. One must read, watch, and engage to maximize one's learning, not exploiting community members as "native informants"—a diminutive role of providing privileged information about a community or cultural group.[25] This goes together with the first tenet of being lifelong learners and being actively involved in one's own educational process.

OUR SHARED RESPONSIBILITY IN ORGANIZATIONS

Acknowledging and neutralizing the privilege payoff ultimately comes down to an essential reality: welcoming and embracing diversity, equity, inclusion, and belonging is a responsibility that all members of our academic communities have. As scholars and practitioners, we have shared expectations for several of the foundational skills that are part of our work: research and teaching, to name two. And while we readily acknowledge that there are those who are particularly gifted in either of these skills, we would not find it acceptable if our colleagues completely "opted out" of teaching or research (though of course there are ways to adjust the balance of both). To be a twenty-first-century academic citizen, we need to add service in creating a welcoming and inclusive campus community to our responsibilities—partly because many of our colleagues do this work disproportionately, and partly because we can better support environments that allow all our members to maximize their potential.

The "passing of the buck" when it comes to equity concerns is both familiar and troubling. For years, I've attended convenings of diversity officers and led professional development sessions at Harvard's Institute for Educational Management with diversity officers, and the refrain is familiar: institutionally, those faculty and administrators of color are expected to wholly take on all matters related to diversity—and woe betide you if your job title actually has the words "multicultural," "diversity," "inclusion," "equity," and/or "belonging" in it. It almost enables our colleagues to walk away from these concerns. The strange irony is, any level of academic or administrative advancement requires *some* exposure to leadership skills, budgeting, human resources, and many other functional areas. However, it's entirely possible to advance as an academic leader with no demonstrated proficiency in diversity, equity, and inclusion. This is rapidly changing, but having expertise and exposure in this domain is seen as being a "plus" rather than being as essential as having experience with budgeting and critical functions.

This is particularly concerning for those of us who work at predominately/historically/traditionally White institutions—as it is a certainty that issues of equity and inclusion need focus on our campuses. I have heard people in these positions—chief diversity officers and directors of multicultural centers, to name two specific roles—express dismay when they, and they alone, are asked and expected to respond to institutional shortcomings related to equity as other administrative leaders look on (perhaps thinking, "There but for the grace of God go I"). When one considers that these roles are almost exclusively held by BIPOC scholars and practitioners, and within, many also hold intersecting marginalized identities (sexuality, social class, ability status, for example), the most pernicious expression of the privilege payoff can have damaging results for the most vulnerable members of our campus communities.

THE MORE YOU KNOW: THE NEXT STEPS AFTER UNDERSTANDING

While I do think that there are those who intentionally exploit the privilege payoff for their own benefit, I suspect that many are unaware that it exists. Like a form of unconscious bias, unless one is reflective and acutely observant of how members of the campus community differently navigate the landscape, the privilege payoff can appear to be "normal" or "just how things are." But with the voluminous evidence that it is indeed real, there are many ways to curtail it.

Dashboards and publicly accessible information about service responsibilities in academia are needed and necessary. Departmental and unit leaders should take the lead in ensuring that at all times, faculty and administrators can know who is, and who is not, carrying the service burden. This is no different than recognizing those who excel in teaching, research, and publishing. Recognizing those who lead in service such as mentoring and advising is another critical step to both acknowledge the work presently done and incentivize it for others. As one colleague of mine said, "It's not like you're going to start mentoring because there's an award or a small bump in your merit pay. But it is nice that someone notices it." Most significantly, it conveys that doing this work won't harm a faculty or staff member.

Just as for our students who are from marginalized communities, being validated matters. Faculty and administrators who are doing significant work on diversity, equity, and inclusion in the institution and community need recognition—particularly from leaders. Most higher education institutions have missions that embrace seeking the truth and contributing to the betterment of society; advancing equity and inclusion fits well within these goals. Moreover, many aspects of what our institutions proclaim as our greatest accomplishments relate to equity concerns. Our research teams are diverse, our performances draw on talents from people of different identities, and so on—part of our responsibility in telling the stories of our accomplishments is ensuring that all those who lent their talents to the work are highlighted. For instance, linking a research team comprised of people of different identities to those who have been working to create a welcoming and inclusive campus climate. This links to the concept of inclusive excellence—*our ability to push the boundaries of knowledge and aspiration is only possible with diverse, thriving, and included people from all backgrounds and identities.*[26] In other words, multicultural and multifaceted campus communities are essential to our institutional achievements.

EMBRACING OUR EQUITY WORK AS STRENGTH

Viewing—and acknowledging—diversity and equity as strengths central to our work is a critical aspect of challenging the privilege payoff and decreasing cultural taxation. It also gives all of us in organizations a common goal—to support all our members, inspire and welcome future members, and work collaboratively so we are all able to contribute free from exhaustion and "leveling up." That way, none of us will be doing significantly more or missing opportunities to relax, restore, spend time with loved ones, or do any of the things we do to be well-rounded and complete human beings.

Now we have clarity that much of the work that advances our institutions comes at considerable psychological and physical cost to many of our colleagues, particularly in this historic moment where we are buffeted by both a viral pandemic and the results of what Reverend Dr. Martin

Luther King, Jr. termed "a poverty of the spirit." [27] We also know that there is significant work needed to address racism, sexism, classism, homophobia, transphobia, ableism, and the intersectional harm visited upon many of our community members. It's also true that some of us hold societal privileges and are able to avoid these consequences—with this knowledge, there is an opportunity to chart a new direction with regard to our institutional spaces. By making these imbalances evident and using interventions supported by research, we can move past hand-wringing and lamentation to action.

Action that is distributed among all in our organizations, not consigned to the individual that has "equity" or "diversity" in their title. We need to make positions that are centered on inclusion sustaining and exciting rather than daunting and exhausting. As a *Chronicle of Higher Education* article noted, the responsibilities of diversity administrators and staff make their positions particularly difficult and tenuous during double pandemics: "It is clear that some job requirements uniquely position DEI workers for burnout. Staff members told me that they were often the first people at their colleges to hold their positions, that they were charged with combating racism even as they experienced it, and that their work sometimes wasn't considered a priority."[28] Further in the article, National Association of Diversity Officers in Higher Education (NADOHE) president Paulette Granberry Russell notes that DEI professionals are expected to shift institutional culture and address issues that are complex and societal. Russell also states how political realities in some states and jurisdictions further have the work of DEI officials in the crosshairs, with bans on the teaching of Critical Race Theory (which rarely has any relation to the academic field of inquiry, but instead intends to chill discourse surrounding race and equity).[29] This development provides yet another way that the privilege payoff favors those from majority identities: again, those in the target sights of bans and other inimicable efforts to silence the voices of marginalized people are also marginalized and minoritized in institutions.

THE ASSAULT ON DIVERSITY, EQUITY, AND INCLUSION: WE ARE THE CASUALTIES

There is another vector of attack, and that is the supposition that universities have byzantine administrative structures and diversity, equity, and inclusion is one of the areas where "administrative bloat" exists.[30] This is a fixation among some observers of higher education, who tend to point out significant salaries and the addition of positions in this area. It's important to note that while there has been a trend of higher education funding declines for years, many states have issued underfunded and unfunded mandates, such as reporting requirements and legislation that fundamentally changes safety and health on college and university campuses.[31] In some instances these mandates have positive intent, but the additional work is shouldered by existing positions—or in some instances, new positions are added.

I find it rare that critiques of the growth of administrative roles are linked to such requirements. Nor do they take into account how policies that impact the day-to-day experiences of survivors of sexual assault, transgender students, and survivors of gun violence, to name some, deepen the need for administrators, staff, and faculty to support these populations. Occasionally, articles critiquing "diversity bureaucracies" enter the media—the *Atlantic* published a provocatively titled story entitled "A Worrisome Peek Inside Yale Law's Diversity Bureaucracy" in October 2021.[32] However, Yale professor Monica Bell raised a number of inaccuracies in the reporting, including the misinformation that the law school had an office of diversity and inclusion, with Bell noting that "there is ONE junior staffer tasked with diversity work in a slightly larger Office of Student Affairs underscores that there is not some large, scary diversity bureaucracy at YLS that is oppressing students. It's just not true."[33]

Diversity officers are often enmeshed in complex problems and disputes, and are easily vilified or identified as "part of the problem." It's little wonder that the scholars/practitioners in these roles report health issues such as stress—especially as many traditionally White institutions of higher education are introducing DEI roles after decades, generations, and even centuries of neglecting equity and inclusion. There is a notable "backlog" of diversity and belonging work that needs to be done, and often it is done by lone individuals or small teams, with a paucity of resources. The sociopolitical and cultural zeitgeist additionally adds another layer of complexity to the work of DEI professionals. The balance sheet tallies more credits to those experiencing the privilege payoff and adds more to the ledger for the culturally taxed. As of late, classrooms, school boards, colleges, and universities are the sites where these nettlesome transactions seem most likely to occur.

CONDUCTING DEI WORK IN THE MORASS OF A MORAL PANIC

The culture wars and moral panic surrounding "political correctness" are not new—I remember the 1993 incident at the University of Pennsylvania where a Jewish male student yelled at a group of Black sorority women and used the epithet "water buffalo."[34] The ensuant accusation of racial harassment, sanctioning, and eventual retraction of the complaint became an issue discussed both in the media and among collegians at the time, especially those of us who were working in student leadership roles during this time.[35] As a master's student and emerging college researcher, I read books like Anne Matthews's *Bright College Years* and found these examinations fascinating but often overblown by a media industry seeking controversy and conflict.[36] Resolution and mediation, it seemed, were not as interesting as inflammatory rhetoric and ad hominems.

I often resist the urge to say, "This is new," but I do sense that the white-hot spotlight on the conflicts and conversations that have been occurring on college campuses marks an increasing intensity surrounding how students, staff, faculty, and the broader community engage—or disengage. There are also savvy provocateurs looking for opportunities to go viral, leveraging the instantaneous reach of social media to distribute audio and video—and using venues for what I call "recreational outrage" to amplify these instances. They exist upon differing plots on the political spectrum, but it does seem that sites such as Campus Reform and the College Fix are particularly successful at producing agitprop that is circulated on social media and sometimes on news pundit shows.

Having my own run-ins with these sites, I question how committed they are to accurately conveying information; instead, they appear to incite anger and accusations of a world gone amok. Indeed, one of the results of the article written about the research that my colleagues and I had conducted was that one of the authors was upbraided by a colleague at her new institution who felt that the term "trauma" was inappropriate outside of war contexts (yes, this really happened). The aesthetic of the story, replete with "scare quotes" and a picture of a disheveled, distressed person, similarly conveys that diversity research is dangerous and threatening.[37] In chapter five, I will discuss how equity and inclusion professionals can do our work while the media spotlight is upon them—but it seems important to note that engaging with media is a task that deserves specific attention, most beneficially from a communications expert. Frequently, a campus incident has precipitating factors, a context, and a plan for response; the media news cycle does not have a parallel structure. Here is another place where those who hold privilege in our environments can leverage their positionality—by interceding and taking on some of the responsibility for communicating to the media, rather than leaving the burden to those who are at the center of the storm, as it were.

DEI professionals need support and partnership from university communicators—and additionally need to proactively build relationships with media, particularly outlets that are invested in responsible and long-form reporting. Many institutions have communications staff who work alongside faculty, administrators, and other staff as partners, identifying responsible media entities to engage with, helping to sharpen our messages to the public, and devising strategies both when we are pushing out stories and when we are responding to campus crises. Building these relationships and having several opportunities to work together, learning what helps communications professionals present our work on inclusivity and equity as well as what helps our communications colleagues understand how we must be intentional in our delivery of our messages, creates the "muscle memory" that is necessary when a media inquiry launches us into action.

If the prior few paragraphs have you thinking, "Wow, diversity and inclusion staff have demanding jobs," I suppose that's half of the takeaway. The other half is that these issues and the requisite media and social engagement around them are intense, partly because DEI professionals are often on an island juggling all of these realities. While it's reasonable to expect leaders in this space to orchestrate, coordinate, and direct efforts, there's also social loafing in equity work, precisely because there can be a learned helplessness for those in higher education spaces—"I'm glad I don't have that job!" When, in fact, that job of creating a more equitable and inclusive working and learning environment is everyone's job. For many of us in the DEI space, the past few years have felt like the scene in *Harry Potter and the Prisoner of Azkaban* when Harry's classmates "volunteer" him to approach Buckbeak . . . by all simultaneously taking a step backward.[38]

WHAT'S NEEDED IN THIS MOMENT

The cadre of professionals in this space have been stretched in unparalleled ways in recent years, given our local, national, and worldwide challenges. Even with progress and hopes for restoring our collective physical, psychological, and societal health, the consequences and trauma of natural and political events will surely be with us, especially for those who hold social, economic, and politically marginalized identities. There is considerable work to be done, and the only sustainable way forward is everybody "mucking in"—all hands on deck.

Those who hold privilege in higher education contexts must acknowledge their positionality and take on some of the weight discussed here and in chapter 3. Equity and inclusion work is the responsibility and privilege of all members of the academic community. It makes us stronger as communities and inspires us to meet our institutional missions as spaces that welcome all. Our present sociocultural and political context requires true allyship; indeed, as some have argued, the stakes are much higher, as we need coconspirators to meet the moment.

CHAPTER FIVE

Wicked Problems

The Role of DEI Leaders in Steering Through Campus Conversations

HIGHER EDUCATION LEADERS will invariably find themselves, their units, or their institutions scrutinized for gaps or absences in how they have attended to diversity, equity, and inclusion issues. This scrutiny can be tied to external events (activism or historical understandings of the university's role in inequitable practices) or internal events (campus climate incidents, institutional debates, and/or institutional changes). In this chapter, I borrow from Rittel and Webber's conceptualization of "wicked problems": ill defined, sprawling, adjacent to unrelated (as well as interconnected) phenomena. Wicked problems elude linear, simplistic solutions; instead, they involve multiple stakeholders and eschew right/wrong formulations, suggesting "better/worse" outcomes. This chapter is a discussion surrounding institutional, departmental, and individual responses to inequity and exclusion on campus. There is a great deal of variance given public/private institutional norms, forms of governance, and institutional temperament; nevertheless, there are useful frameworks that can aid institutional leaders in formulating responses, such as a typology of campus cultural orientations that can assist leaders in understanding their particular campus context.

Moving to a practitioner orientation, I will intersperse my experiences as a faculty member in the Harvard Programs in Professional Education instructing, advising, and learning from institutional leaders navigating DEI issues. In this practitioner/scholar space, we are often asked for "three things to do," which takes the conceptual and scholarly knowledge to the practical and immediate. While referencing these foundational theories, the intent is to provide pragmatic and actionable strategies and steps to effectively engage campus constituencies moving forward.

Having just emerged from a campus controversy that is evolving into a conversation—one which garnered a multiplicity of concerns on climate, imagery, athletics, and the era of racial reckoning sparked by the murder of George Floyd in May 2020—this chapter will also feature "notes from the field," where I provide perspectives of engaging, and sometimes leading dialogue across generations, among faculty, staff, students, and alumni, and with the broader public. An honest discussion will also present the more challenging aspects of DEI discussions, particularly engaging with those inimical and even hostile to forthright immersion on race and identity—which is exacerbated by a reactionary and siloed political climate. Dialogue is further complicated by an unnuanced social media environment that fails to amplify, magnify, and clarify—which instead further balkanizes and stakes out more extreme, less engaged positions. As we close, I will endorse approaches that bring communities together in dialogue, no matter how dissonant, in an effort to find common ground—even if that space of understanding is as essential as "we agree that this institution is worth fighting for."

EXCLUSION AND INEQUITY: WOVEN INTO THE FABRIC OF PREDOMINANTLY WHITE INSTITUTIONS

I've often argued that predominantly, traditionally, and historically White institutions inherently have issues pertaining to histories of exclusion. In the United States, this tracks with the nation's own troubled history of

Native American genocide and land theft, the enslavement of African people brought to North America as chattel, and many other forms of discrimination toward immigrants, LGBTQIA people, people with disabilities, people of diverse faith traditions, and those from working-class and poor families. The very attributes that made these institutions "shining cities on a hill" are in essence the troublesome origins and aspects of the colleges and universities in which many of us work, teach, and learn. In short, difficulties and controversies pertaining to diversity, equity, inclusion, and belonging aren't, to borrow from the lingua franca of computer programmers, a bug at most institutions—they're a feature.[1]

Too often, equity-focused crises at PWIs are viewed as "black swan" events—unexpected aberrations of culture and norms—when in fact, they are very much the fabric of American colleges and universities.[2] How those black swans appear, however, can vary. Sometimes, there is a well-known history of exclusion during its founding that is part of the institution's origin story, which might have been heralded in a different time, but in the twentieth and twenty-first century is noxious and offensive. Questions surrounding how institutions were founded, the political and moral stances of institutional founders and leaders, how communities were disrupted by institutions, and how policies and procedures, both de jure and de facto, prohibited access and inclusion to colleges and universities are all part of the inward reflection that we should have the courage to initiate and engage with.

One of the most significant examples of inward reflection was led by Dr. Ruth Simmons, who became the first Black woman to lead an Ivy League institution when she was inaugurated as president of Brown University in Rhode Island in 2001. In 2003, President Simmons appointed a committee of faculty, students, and administrators, tasking them with uncovering and documenting Brown University's ties to the slave trade in Rhode Island and across North America. Simmons's courage inspired other institutions in the Ivy League and across American higher education to engage in similar research—indeed, the recent report on Harvard

University's ties to slavery acknowledges Simmons's leadership in this area.[3] The foundational text linking American colonial universities to chattel slavery and the exploitation, abuse, and denigration of African and Native American people is Dr. Craig Steven Wilder's *Ebony and Ivy: Race, Slavery, and the Troubled History of America's Universities*—a book I assign parts of in my history of higher education course.[4] Simmons and Wilder prompted many universities to face the reckoning with their histories with slavery and exploitation: the consortium of Universities Studying Slavery (USS), led by the University of Virginia, numbers ninety-four members, including American, Canadian, Irish, and British universities, and Historically Black Colleges and Universities (HBCUs).[5]

While participation in slavery is one of the most egregious examples of how universities and colleges have exploited and betrayed the ideals of truth and humanity, there are regrettably many others. Higher education institutions are reflections of the social and political realities of the communities and the policy contexts in which they were formed. This is the reason why reflection and historical evaluation of our institutions' origin are needed and essential, as institutions that espouse the pursuit of knowledge, no matter where it leads. Knowing one's history is one thing, but deciding what to do with it once painful and problematic truths are (un)/(re)covered is entirely another. I will use this chapter to discuss some approaches, many of them grounded in my own experience helming one such investigation at the University of Texas at Austin.

THE WICKED PROBLEMS OF RECKONING WITH INEQUITY

In responding to the question "What next?" I am reminded of a theory I encountered in a course I co-taught with my colleagues Dr. Julia Mickenberg and Kate Catterall. Coming from distinct academic traditions—American studies and design, respectively, and my own grounding in educational research—we found ourselves reading new ideas as we shaped a course on the history and future of higher education. From the realm of design, Kate introduced me to the work of design theorist Horst Rittel, who with Melvin Webber theorized *wicked problems*.[6] Rittel and Webber center their work around architectural and design challenges, but I found it to be a useful framework for the issues we were confronting in higher education institutions.

In 1973, Rittel and Webber acknowledged the advances of professionals in city planning, social work, and health, noting their success in solving "easy" problems, noting that professionals were "turning our attention to others that are much more stubborn."[7] This is perhaps most clearly explained in this passage: "One reason the publics have been attacking the social professions, we believe, is that the cognitive and occupational styles of the professions—mimicking the cognitive style of science and the occupational style of engineering—have just not worked on a wide array of social problems."[8] Technical-rational approaches, those that would address a health crisis or housing dilemma, do not consider our morality, our subjective worldviews, and our concerns with equity. Rittel and Webber contrast mathematical computation with the placement of a highway or school curricula—lacking the clarifying traits we see in scientific processes. Indeed, even identifying the wicked problem creates a problem. Wicked problems can be categorized in the following ways:

1. There is no definitive formulation of a wicked problem.
2. Wicked problems have no stopping rule.
3. Solutions to wicked problems are not true-or-false, but good-or-bad.
4. There is no immediate and no ultimate test of a solution to a wicked problem.
5. Every solution to a wicked problem is a "one-shot operation"; because there is no opportunity to learn by trial-and-error, every attempt counts significantly.
6. Wicked problems do not have an enumerable (or an exhaustively describable) set of potential solutions, nor is there a well-described

set of permissible operations that may be incorporated into the plan.

7. Every wicked problem is essentially unique.
8. Every wicked problem can be considered to be a symptom of another problem.
9. The existence of a discrepancy representing a wicked problem can be explained in numerous ways. The choice of explanation determines the nature of the problem's resolution.
10. The planner has no right to be wrong.[9]

Rittel and Webber note that postindustrial societies—more diverse and comprised of different groups—often see solutions that are radically divergent from each other. Without a unifying social goal, it's impossible to satisfy all in our society—thus the dilemma of the wicked problem.

While Rittel and Webber's observations from fifty years ago carry significant weight, it could be argued that we are moving toward large portions of the population supporting some solutions. Quinnipiac University's 2020 poll revealed that a majority of Americans support removing Confederate statues from public spaces, support renaming military bases named after Confederate leaders, and see the Confederate flag as a symbol of racism.[10] (One demographic, Republican-identifying respondents, had a majority reporting the opposite.) So for colleges and universities with such imagery, this issue is moving toward "easy" in the Rittel/Webber conceptualization—with the caveat that the margins on these issues are closer in the southern United States. The University of Texas at Austin removed Confederate statues from the center of campus in 2017, as did the city of New Orleans, and Richmond, Virginia, the former capital of the Confederacy, which removed statues from Monument Avenue in 2020.[11]

A more wicked version of this campus equity and inclusion issue would be dealing with buildings named for individuals who lived during the Confederacy or the Jim Crow era—some individuals may be deemed worthy of the honor, and others may not. This provides an opportunity for institutions of higher education to engage in what we do best—an examination of history, context, and engaging individuals from different perspectives in the inquiry. I had an opportunity to engage in this work during the 2020–2021 academic year at my institution.

I am a member of a distinct group of faculty in higher education—a "homecomer" in the faculty ranks. I became interested in this the day I was offered a tenure-track position at the University of Texas at Austin—the institution I had attended as an undergraduate—as an "accidental cluster hire" with Dr. Victor Sáenz, in 2007. We were unique in our context, but we had colleagues across the nation who were also homecomers, and we even held a conference panel on our experiences.[12] The only example we could find of a faculty member's reflection on teaching at and navigating the institution they had attended from late adolescence to adulthood was P. F. Kluge's *Alma Mater: A College Homecoming*, detailing the novelist's return to Kenyon College as an English professor. Eventually, Victor and I realized that our shared experience and additional complexities as men of color navigating a historically White institution as tenure-track faculty would be an interesting scholarly inquiry, and we published a paper in the *Harvard Educational Review*.[13] In the article, I mused over the Du Boisian double consciousness that is inherently part of attending, loving, and questioning a historically White institution:

> On graduation, I brought honor and acclaim to my community and the university by being selected as a student marshal and a distinguished graduate. But my relationship with UT Austin was complex. On the one hand, it was a site of great opportunities, mentorship, and learning. On the other, I felt that the shadow of discrimination still graced the 40 Acres, witnessed in the statues of Confederate officials still standing on the South Mall of campus and the actions of conservative student groups that insisted the presence of students of color was due only to affirmative action. UT Austin's troubled racial

history ensured my confusion over whether the institution was truly respectful not only of me, but also of my family and friends in southeast Austin, who often viewed the campus as another world. To be a Longhorn—to "get my Horns up," as the TV ads exhorted UT Austin students and alumni to do—did I have to put down my cultural and social values?[14]

ALL EYES ON ME: CONSIDERING AND CONFRONTING "THE EYES OF TEXAS"

One example of this double consciousness related to UT Austin's alma mater, "The Eyes of Texas." The first I had heard of this controversy was in 2009, when I read an article that discussed both the melody (from the folk song "I've Been Working on the Railroad") and the initial performance of the song at a minstrel show, presumably in blackface, in 1903.[15] Initially I was surprised at the revelation; but a review of the university's traditions—which I had assiduously studied as an orientation advisor and member of spirit organizations—verified the origins at the minstrel show.[16] I'm not sure why our various groups that were engaged on issues of social justice overlooked the origin of the song, but we had. Indeed, I had taken a course on the music of Black Americans during my undergraduate days at UT and remembered reading the section on minstrelsy in Ellen Southern's *The Music of Black Americans*—seems like it should have come up there![17]

The summer of 2020 had a baleful start. While watching a report about Christian Cooper, the Black birder who was harassed by a White woman while birding in Central Park, I first heard the name George Floyd. When the horror of his murder unfolded, I was uncharacteristically mute. I had been leveraging my position as a researcher to comment on sociocultural issues via public scholarship for some time, writing for *CNN Opinion*, *Fortune*, and many of the major dailies in the state of Texas. However, I was utterly devastated after witnessing George Floyd's life expire via a police officer's knee to his neck for nearly nine minutes. I was particularly broken after talking to my then twelve-year-old son Karl about George Floyd, and my realization that I had been talking to him about the extralegal deaths of Black people more or less since he had started school—Philando Castile, Sandra Bland, and so many others. Coinciding with this, the older Generation Z populace—college students—were viewing George Floyd's death as a critical moment to advocate for the social justice concerns central to the Black Lives Matter movement.

In June 2020, a group of UT Austin student athletes issued a statement demanding changes in the UT athletic department. The demands were posted on social media and included donating 0.5 percent of the department's annual earnings to the Black Lives Matter movement and Black organizations, establishing a permanent Black athletic history exhibit in the UT Athletics Hall of Fame, and renaming parts of the football stadium after Julius Whittier, the first Black football letterman at UT Austin. Their demands also went beyond the athletics department, with additional demands to rename campus buildings named after segregationists, require a module on the history of racism at UT, increase outreach in the urban areas of the state, and discontinue the school song, "The Eyes of Texas."[18]

I recalled a student petition that had amassed thousands of signatures demanding the changing of several campus buildings and "acknowledg[ing] the racist roots of 'The Eyes of Texas' and its origins from a reoccurring minstrel show on campus through a formal statement to the student body."[19] My colleague and Black Studies department chair Dr. Ted Gordon had conducted a racial geography tour of the UT campus for many years, and in fact regularly led my history of higher education classes on the tour. The energy around confronting and discussing UT's history, particularly around racism and exclusion, was at a peak. I engaged in some discussions with the athletics department, directly speaking with student athletes, alums, and administrators, as well as with our alumni association—as a professor, alum, and scholar of higher education and student resistance, I could bring perspectives about how other institutions had grappled with similar issues.

Indeed, UT Austin had undergone several racially transformational experiences in the years I had been a student and a faculty member. In the 1990s, in response to racist incidents from members of the Greek community and a lack of recognition of Black leaders, a movement started to erect a statue of the Reverend Dr. Martin Luther King, Jr. on campus. Indeed, my peers and I voted in a referendum to allocate some of our student fees to the statue.[20] In 2007, UT Austin established a Division of Diversity and Community Engagement (DDCE), where I was a faculty fellow and eventually an assistant vice president.[21] Perhaps most visibly, the statues of Confederate leaders that had been prominently erected on the South Mall of campus were removed in 2017, following a report from a committee chaired by then vice president of DDCE, Dr. Gregory Vincent.[22] We had also confronted the issue of renaming buildings, with a residence hall named for a prominent UT Law professor—who was also a cofounder of the Ku Klux Klan in Florida—being renamed in 2010.[23] As a postbellum university in the South, the examples of campus symbols and ephemera that hold connections to the Confederacy and the Jim Crow era surround this campus.

This was all happening as UT Austin was undergoing an unprecedented change in leadership. In April 2020, we learned that both our president Greg Fenves and provost Maurie McInnis—both of whom I considered to be supportive and strong advocates for equity and inclusion—were departing UT Austin for presidencies at Emory and Stony Brook, respectively.[24] The dean of the UT Austin business school, Jay Hartzell, was appointed as interim president. While I didn't know Hartzell, I knew that helming an institution during a pandemic would be a significant challenge.

After the student athletes' statement and demands became public, there was increased interest in what the institutional response would be, not only from the students themselves but from a multitude of other constituents: the larger student body, alums, UT faculty and staff, and the media. My own review of the facts at hand left me thinking that many of the demands were thoughtfully laid out, and in fact, were being worked on. I knew, for instance, that we had outreach centers in Houston and Dallas as well as other parts of the state—to be a UT presence in those cities. I had been on calls with the student athlete council where the athletic director, Chris Del Conte, updated the students on the funding of initiatives discussed in the statement. It seemed to me that the 2020–2021 year would be a tumultuous one, and my history of higher education course would be a great place for us to discuss many of the relevant issues related to the growing discussion on equity and inclusion.

STEPPING INTO THE UNKNOWN: LEADING THE RESEARCH EFFORT

In September 2020, I received a call from President Hartzell's office; Would I be available to meet? I eagerly agreed, recalling that I had been invited to share my thoughts with the prior two presidents, Bill Powers and Greg Fenves, in prior years. My perspectives as an alum, a faculty member who studied DEI in higher education, and a campus leader on issues of equity related to students were, in my opinion, helpful for institutional leaders. I read President Hartzell's statement, released just a few days after the release of the demands, pledging to listen to concerns and then to create "a plan this summer to address these issues, do better for our students and help overcome racism."[25] At the end of our discussion, which had already reached into the early evening, President Hartzell asked if I would be interested in serving on a committee examining the issues around "The Eyes of Texas." I said yes—considering the multiple identities that I held, some of which would no doubt conflict with having a sense of belonging and inclusion in the campus community, I honestly did not think this was a conversation I could, or wanted to, avoid.

Early the next week, President Hartzell called with a follow up question: Considering our conversation, would I be interested in serving as the chair of the committee investigating "The Eyes of Texas?" My stomach sank instantly. I knew I wanted no part of either killing or officially giving life back to the alma mater. Who would? I asked the president about this, and he reminded me that he had stated in July 2020 that the song would remain.[26] Instead, this committee would focus on four charges:

1. Collect and document the facts of the origin, the creators' intent, and the elements of "The Eyes of Texas," including the lyrics and music.
2. Examine the university's historical institutional use and performance of "The Eyes of Texas."
3. Chronicle the historical usage of "The Eyes of Texas" by University of Texas students, staff, faculty, and alumni, as well as its usage in broader cultural events, such as film, literature, and popular media.
4. Recommend potential communication tactics and/or strategies to memorialize the history of "The Eyes of Texas."[27]

One of the lessons I have learned and impart to others is "never make a split-second decision on something that will consume significant hours of your life." I asked for a day to consult with mentors, all of whom thought that while this would be a challenging task, my experience and interests made me a natural fit for it. I even reached out to the vice president for diversity and community engagement to make sure that my leading the committee would not obstruct his leadership; I received his blessing. I was also encouraged by the fact that the work on "The Eyes of Texas" was part of a continual reflection of our university's historical rooting in exclusion and our willingness to confront it—with plans to commemorate and honor our first Black students, including Heman Marion Sweatt, the plaintiff in the landmark *Sweatt v. Painter* Supreme Court case that led to the integration of UT Austin.[28] Systemic changes, as articulated in strategic planning, are essential to ensure that the responses to inequity are not *ad hoc*, but rather aligned to institutional priorities.

With these endorsements and this support, I was excited to embark on this work from the perspective of a scholar and of an alum and a member of the UT Austin community. President Hartzell and I agreed that the committee would need to be diverse, yet relatively small, to be efficient. We settled on "no more than 25" and compiled a list of alums, students, faculty, and staff who were involved in athletics, spirit organizations, the Longhorn Band, and campus leadership. Within those categories, we sought individuals from diverse backgrounds—age, race, ethnicity, gender, and so on. While it would be impossible to represent the full complexity of 540,000 living alums and 51,000 students, we felt the committee was a mosaic of the UT Austin community.

Virtually everybody we invited to the committee expressed gratitude—and immediately asked for clarification for the duties of the committee. Like me, most people were extremely unwilling to be the arbiters of the song's continuation or cancellation. When we clarified the charges, most of the people we invited enthusiastically agreed to join our work. There were a few who let us know that they would not be able to serve, but I was impressed that many people were willing to help—without compensation, during a pandemic, where most of us were working and teaching remotely and trying to balance life through Zoom and family disruptions.

I immediately felt out of my depth with this responsibility. Because the appointment came in September, I was already teaching my fall history course. There were not additional resources in the form of time, though I did negotiate funding support for my graduate research assistants and scheduler to assist with our work. President Hartzell introduced me to Brad Deutser, a business consultant, creative strategist, and executive coach.[29] Brad was working with the university on a multitude of issues, including creating more opportunities for belonging and assisting with "The Eyes of Texas" research project. I didn't know it at the time, but Brad would become a close friend and trusted confidant who helped me immensely as I led our committee. I could count on Brad for advice and as a sounding board—but he always reminded me, "This is your committee. Whatever your decision, I'll support you." Brad embarked on interviews with many members of the UT Austin community—band members, athletes, and resource groups. I think by the end, Brad had met with over 300 groups of students, staff, faculty, and alums.

FINDING COMMON PURPOSE AND PURSUIT

Our initial challenge was to create a sense of connection and common purpose with our committee. We didn't have the ability to meet in person, so we had to build community virtually. We also knew very little about each member's personal stance regarding the song—which in some ways was ideal. It meant that we never assumed that the group had a particular mindset. Brad helped us create an anonymous survey of our prior knowledge about "The Eyes of Texas" and our personal feelings about the song. While the survey revealed that some members passionately wanted the song retired, and some wanted the song retained, most of our committee expressed curiosity and inquiry as their leading perspectives. They wanted to learn more and engage with different ideas and viewpoints.

Every Thursday from November until January, I hopped on a Zoom with the committee immediately after my history class. We came together from across the state, Florida, and even the next day in Singapore. Initially we were all getting a sense of each other, but soon the networks started to grow—people found connections through other members and, of course, shared experiences at the university. That doesn't mean we didn't encounter conflict, both individually and as a group. My leadership and organizational theory training presented the realization that we were going to encounter rifts—How would we deal with them? I knew the most important thing was to embrace that this work was inherently controversial and that we would not always agree. So, we established norms about how we would work together—but what was evident immediately was that there was immense respect for the people in the group. Student leaders, world class athletes, distinguished scholars, and talented artists came together and *listened*. We honored silence and hearing from each other.

UNDER THE BRIGHT LIGHTS: CONTROVERSY AND MEDIA

One aspect of the committee work that I was both unfamiliar and uncomfortable with was the intense media interest in our work. Upon reflection, I can understand how big-time collegiate athletics, a racial controversy, and a Black man as the leader of the committee would make an intriguing story. I fully expected our local and even statewide media to be interested in the story, but when ESPN, the *Washington Post*, *Time*, and the *New York Times* began to focus on the story, it became larger than anything I'd imagined. J. B. Bird, UT Austin's director of media relations and issues management, was the recipient of many phone calls and texts from me. While many in the media were diligent, some were less careful. Our work, the four charges, was being conflated with the decision to retain the song as well as other dynamics in collegiate athletics and racial politics.

I realized I was fighting an impossible battle: wanting to explain the work in detail when most media outlets wanted ten seconds; wanting to acknowledge that as a Black man it might seem as if I could be positioned as a convenient "fig leaf" for a predominantly White institution's racist past. *We're not racist! See, we have a Black guy leading this committee!* None of these "hot takes" considered my deep involvement at the university as a student, as a member of spirit organizations, and a scholar of higher education who specifically taught courses at the intersection of racial equity, history, and student activism—I honestly believed that my experiences were strongly suited to engage in this work.

I was not naive about what it meant to be, in the most irresponsible interpretation, representing the university in seeming opposition to student activists who wanted to change the status quo. A football season marked by a losing streak, punctuated by a story alleging that the team's quarterback had been abandoned by his teammates as he sang "The Eyes of Texas" once again thrust our committee in the spotlight, even though our work had no bearing on the song's performance, and in fact, other players were singing the song in other parts of the field.[30] More stories came out alleging that alums were organizing to keep "The Eyes of Texas," particularly focusing on racist comments sent to the president's email account.[31] Each time these stories broke, I was usually asked to comment. I felt that I was an unwilling participant in the whims of news departments. At the same time, J. B. and I worked with several reporters who gave us time and simultaneously understood that not every development required a story.

This represented one of the times when your research and rhetoric runs directly into your life. Was I being tokenized? Exploited? Culturally taxed? I remember being exhausted and depressed because our efforts and work were being reduced to "the university committee, led by Rich Reddick, is working in opposition to social justice." What sustained me, though, were the wonderful friendships I have had over the years—and the ones I forged during our work. The phone calls and texts from friends—even those I didn't know well—simply saying "I got your back," or discussing aspects of the work. My colleagues, who reached out with research tips or information that would suit our work, kindly thought of our committee and wanted to help our work be the best it could be.

A project this significant has to have a public-facing aspect, even during a global pandemic. During our research, we had a web portal that allowed people to share their experiences and information about "The Eyes of Texas." Thousands of messages flooded in—people sharing how the song was part of their lives, how it was played at weddings, funerals, and other life transitions. We also heard from people that said the song didn't have that sense for them, and how they felt the university was overlooking their concerns. For the most part, the messages were respectful, and I appreciated how people could express their views civilly and support the work of the committee. Every so often, there would be a message that suggested that our work was to decide whether the song would remain the alma mater or not, despite our consistent communication and reference to President Hartzell's decision months earlier to retain the song. I was additionally interested in the number of letters that came in from people who were neither alums nor people with a formal affiliation to the university.

In addition, we consulted with several people outside of the committee based on their specialized knowledge. We met with Dianne Boddy and Jeanne Klein, the granddaughters of Lewis Johnson, one of the instigators of "The Eyes of Texas." We had a meeting with Michael Ray Charles, the Rome Prize-winning artist whose work confronts racial stereotypes and slavery, and heard from Dr. Charles Carson, a colleague and acclaimed musicologist. A group of us met with student athletes, primarily from the football team, to hear about their experiences with disrespectful fans during the season. Outside of our meetings, each subcommittee worked independently to respond to the charges set by President Hartzell. I was continually impressed with the time and effort our collective applied to the work, as we balanced work, family, and pandemic life.

As our research concluded, I worked with a small subcommittee to complete our writing. Like every other group project in 2020–2021, we needed additional time to finish, which we were granted by President Hartzell. A friend alerted me that a UT fan message board had been tracking the work of the committee, from the announcement of our committee to each story that appeared in the media. I got a glimpse of what our student athletes and university administrators often dealt with—claims that my personal biases, research agenda, and personal scholarship would prevent me from chairing the committee effectively. One message was simply my faculty profile picture—dreadlocked and in a dashiki—with the words, "OH NO."[32] For the most part I was unbothered by the commentary, recalling the words of Kipling's poem "If": "If you can wait and not be tired by waiting / Or, being lied about, don't deal in lies, / Or, being hated, don't give way to hating, / And yet don't look too good, nor talk too wise."[33]

Every so often a poster who claimed to know me would present a contrasting perspective, but it reminded me of the first advice I had received from my mentor and coauthor Greg Vincent on the occasion of our first op-ed being published in the *Austin American-Statesman*: "Congratulations, and do yourself a favor . . . don't read the comments."[34] And of course, I did. It was interesting to see what connections people drew to our work with the cloak of internet anonymity.

RELEASING OUR WORK TO THE WORLD

At long last, our report was completed in February 2021. I sent the one-hundred-page draft to President Hartzell for his review. I really didn't know what to expect. If the thought was that the report would be a Potemkin village for "The Eyes of Texas" and UT Austin's history, we certainly did not deliver. We discussed the absence of Black people at the university, the lynchings and racial violence in the county in the early twentieth century, and the racism experienced by Black students not just as the first "Precursors" arrived on campus in the 1950s but more recently from the football coaching staff in the 1970s. We also presented how the song swiftly shifted from a parody potentially performed in blackface at a minstrel show in 1903 to a solemn hymn commemorating a president two years later—and its use as a protest song from the earliest days until the 1970s.[35] Our committee, replete with four tenured historians, several academics, and a broad representation of campus experiences, was both proud and relieved. But I also worried—What would happen if we were asked to change or edit part of the report? The committee firmly felt that our university needed to confront the truth, no matter how jarring or disappointing it might be. I needn't have worried; several days later, President Hartzell replied with a note of thanks and said the report was ready for release—with no changes or edits.

The following week was a flurry of back and forths with the UT communication team as they formatted, typeset, and inserted photos into the document. At long last, we informed the media and campus community that the report would be released on March 9, 2021. We also had to create an executive summary, which I understood, but also caused me concern because I knew some people would immediately read those eight pages and assume that they would convey the complexity of the research. (They would not.) March 9 started with a meeting with student athletes in the morning, several press interviews, and ten-to-fifteen-minute sessions with student groups, alumni groups, and other members of the UT community. I'm not sure how we did it, but I don't recall being that tired since the birth of my youngest. At the end of the day, I felt a sense of relief—naively believing that the majority of the work was over.

I have intentionally decided not to delve into significant detail regarding the findings of our committee's work—they exist in report and multimedia form at https://eyesoftexas.utexas.edu. However, one important question arose surrounding the lyrics of "The Eyes of Texas." There was significant confusion about the origin of the lyrics—Were they derived from a favorite saying of Robert E. Lee, "The eyes of the South are upon you?" Did they have to do with surveillance of Black people in any way? From our research, we were very certain that the lyrics referenced the words of President Prather, from both the now unsung verse that follows the familiar song that starts with the lyric, "Sing me a song of Prexy . . ." and the notes of Lewis Johnson and John Lang Sinclair.[36] It was also not inspired by the words of Robert E. Lee, as we could find no record of Lee uttering the phrase "The eyes of the South are upon you." We felt we could correct the historical record about the lyrical intent and carefully worded our findings:

> The research leads us to surmise that the intent of "The Eyes of Texas" was not overtly racist. However, it is similarly clear that the cultural milieu that produced it was. And the fact that the song was,

> for decades, sung and revered on a segregated campus has, understandably, blurred the lines between intent and historical and contemporary impact. This complicates its understanding and explains how different people experienced the song in vastly different ways.[37]

We soon found out that this paragraph would be abridged to only the first sentence—many articles appeared that either omitted the entire remaining paragraph or barely mentioned the sentence confirming that the milieu of a postbellum, Jim Crow university, city, and state were in fact mired in racism, and the campus's segregated past further solidified this reality.

SOUND BITES AND CONVENIENT QUOTES: (DIS)ENGAGING WITH THE RESEARCH

The fact that some focused on one sentence and attempted to distill months of research and writing into sixteen words was easily the most frustrating aspect of the process. We acknowledged that we could only unearth so much with few sources and very few primary sources at our disposal—but a committee of historians and scholars could agree on the contents of our research, which reflected truths, difficult and admirable, related to the school song. Upon reflection, I realize that some people wanted a simple answer to a complex historical inquiry, and our report was not going to satisfy those who wanted "a cudgel to settle a debate."[38]

Most hurtful were the accusations of some that the report was a form of "gaslighting." I simply submit that anyone reading the over 30,000-word document could not come to such a conclusion. For weeks, a faculty colleague independently released a report that purported to debunk our research. I found this interesting, as so many faculty colleagues had reached out with information and leads to assist in our work—I learned of this "minority report" from members of the media, while the faculty member's announcement came hours after the first press inquiry. While nobody's research—including our own—is above reproach, the antagonistic and adversarial nature of one person's interpretation of history, compared to a report from a multitude of scholars who painstakingly reviewed both the archival data and writing, seemed at odds with truly working toward an honest appraisal of the truth.

Occasionally I would receive an email from one faculty colleague first asking, then demanding, that I participate in a forum to debate the findings of the report. I had no interest in this; our report was available for the community to review, and I saw this as an attempt to elevate another agenda. Furthermore, I resented having my time hijacked at the whim of another—over half a year of intense focus on the report was enough. I appreciated that one of our committee members sat on one of these panels, and as our work was now released, we all had the ability to speak on it as coauthors. However, with the exception of a few colleagues with whom I had promised to discuss the project previously, I was most interested in returning to some sense of normalcy—my own teaching and scholarship.

I knew many of the students centrally involved in the issues surrounding "The Eyes of Texas" before the committee and the report, and I was happy to talk with them about our process and what we had learned. These conversations, including those that started with very strong feelings, were cathartic. Never once did I expect anyone to change their perspective, but more often the outcome was an understanding that it was possible to look at a 120-year-old artifact and assess its impact in different ways. Certainly, that is what our committee found. I also had a particular appreciation for those who took the time to read the report and raise questions about our interpretation of certain elements.

TIME AND SPACE FOR ENGAGEMENT

Eventually, with the white-hot media focus fading, it became possible to discuss the committee and my involvement more rationally. I was invited by faculty colleagues to discuss our work as a case study in leadership, crisis management, and diversity, equity, inclusion, and belonging. I often had to preface these discussions by explaining that there were many more constituents and leaders involved in the work, so they were getting only a slice of what had occurred. But ultimately these were the most revelatory discussions I have had the privilege of having. The student questions often had me thinking at a deeper level and appreciating their concerns. UT Austin students (as well as those at Southwestern University and at the Harvard Graduate School of Education, where I have also spoken about the committee and our work) are brilliant, inquisitive, and ask thoughtful questions; I learn a lot from their perspectives.

Because of the community interest in our work, I still have people occasionally reaching out at events to express their views about "The Eyes of Texas." These engagements are generally very positive, and I am humbled by the appreciation that people have for the work of the committee. We all worked very hard on the report, at a time when most of us had more demands than ever regarding our families and our work. It speaks to the kinds of people who comprised our committee—committed, with an incredible sense of fairness and making our community a better place. I made lifelong friends in this process, and a constellation of mentors and confidants that I still access for advice on many dilemmas.

REFLECTING ON THE CHAOS: CONSIDERING THE PERSONAL IMPACT

I also can appreciate why some leaders would elect *not* to participate or lead an effort like this one. There is a level of cultural taxation that is significant, and frankly, the media focus can exacerbate it. We intentionally told my story of student to professor to the public, so it would instill the reality that I was leading this work not only as a scholar but also as a member of the community with a deep commitment to how our community would fare during and after our work was complete. It was also possible to derive, ascribing the worst possible motives, that I was interested in self-promotion and career advancement. In fact, I heard this directly from some critics who thought I should not have participated in this project. These accusations were hurtful, and I regularly consulted with my circle of mentors and advisors to ask "Was that the right decision?" Again, having that circle of confidants—many of whom hold marginalized identities—was fundamental for me. All folks who work in diversity and equity roles need such circles, not just on our discrete campuses but across the nation and world. In many ways, the only people who can relate to residing in the eye of the hurricane are those who have been similarly tested or might be tested in the future.

I realized that some of my mentors and friends dealt with what I had experienced for a year more or less daily as part of their jobs. Operating in the liminal space of advancing equity and inclusion—and advocating for the voices of those on the margins—can be thankless, as some will see you as a pawn or sellout. The strategies of sitting down with those with different viewpoints, finding convergences of outcomes, and expressing resistance in spaces where nobody is watching require a commitment to what organizational theorist Dr. Debra Meyerson calls "change, the quiet way."[39]

The colleagueship and community of those who operate with only a few degrees of freedom has been invaluable in my career. Foregrounding diversity, inclusion, and equity at traditionally/historically/predominantly White institutions is the very definition of a "wicked problem." As I once told a reporter, we are often attempting to craft solutions to problems that American society has yet to figure out. As a participant and observer in higher education my entire adult life, my appreciation for those people who are committed to the work is immense. Our institutional, community, and political environments can be radically different, and sometimes it takes time to find the place that fits us, and vice versa. Permanent discomfort might be the inevitable outcome, but one becomes acclimated to discomfort. Sometimes.

A TYPOLOGY OF CAMPUS CULTURES

One framework that is useful in gauging our institutional capacity for examination and change was developed by my friends and fellow higher education researchers Drs. Uma Jayakumar and Sam Museus. In their book *Creating Campus Cultures*, they conceptualize a typology of campus cultures that demonstrates "how they can work to transform the cultures on their campuses to maximize success among racially diverse student bodies."[40]

The categories are (1) Eurocentric, which are institutions with racially and ethnically homogeneous campus cultures that neither voice diversity values, nor do those values exist among students, conversations, and decisions on the campus; (2) diversity-oriented—institutions with espoused and limited enactment of diversity values with this cultural orientation and these values manifest among students, conversations, decision-making, and curricula; and (3) at the apex, equity-oriented—institutions with cultures that recognize the pervasive nature of institutional and structural racism, exclusionary institutional practices (past and present), and recognize that the experiences and knowledge of White, middle- and upper-class students are frequently valued over those of students of color, and are cognizant that this occurs. In the equity-oriented campus culture, historically marginalized populations are involved and active in decision-making, governance, and discourse throughout the campus, in a noncompartmentalized manner.[41]

What I have found, as Jayakumar and Museus state, is that "college campuses have operated in a relatively fragmented way"—I can certainly traverse parts of our campus that fit all three categories.[42] This was certainly the case during the research around "The Eyes of Texas." While different constituencies—with different levers and kinds of power—could claim Eurocentric, diversity-oriented, and equity-oriented identities, we truly interacted with a wide range of perspectives and types of engagement. In the aggregate, however, in my opinion, my campus has an emerging diversity-oriented campus culture. I also believe that this framework is assuaged by the sociopolitical context surrounding the campus—one seen particularly at public institutions where state governments and boards exert both explicit and hidden control over governance.

In recent years, as reactionary state governments have assumed power and declared colleges and universities as battlegrounds in moral panics and culture wars, I have heard more campus leaders state that they must filter best practices through the political realities in their locales. Some of the efforts that would advance equitable outcomes and address disparities in opportunities, experiences, and outcomes would both make intriguing battlegrounds for those stoking divisive culture skirmishes—and cause criticism that would ultimately blunt the efficacy of these efforts, even hurting the students who are most at risk. Regrettably, we can already see how some marginalized populations are weathering withering scrutiny because political actors have scapegoated them in their craven attempts to curry favor with some constituents.

My colleague Dr. Robbin Chapman, who cochairs the Harvard Program in Professional Education Bravely Confronting Racism, and I often hear our participants ask, "How do we commit to the practices and programs that will move our campus closer to equity, when the political environments in which we work figure so greatly in what we are able to do regarding resource allocation and institutional attention?" This is not an easy question to answer. However, there are strategies that I propose that may augment these challenging realities that many of our students, administrators, and faculty are facing. In chapter 6, I will frame what restorative resistance looks like, on the individual and structural level. In this decade, our work toward equity may look different in comparison to prior eras where there may have been a greater embrace of efforts to equalize opportunity and outcomes.

The example I've shared in this chapter of presenting a wicked problem in diversity, equity, and inclusion, and discussing efforts to confront and advance our collective knowledge and engagement on the issue, may well be happening on your campus, or be on its way. I hope these reflections can assist your work going forward. Just know you'll have lots to process and reflect on as it happens, and after.

CHAPTER SIX

Restorative Resistance

A Sustainable Path Forward for DEI Leaders at All Levels

FBI DIRECTOR CHRISTOPHER WRAY'S 2020 declaration that White supremacist terrorism constituted a majority of US domestic terrorism threats may have been shocking to some, but historically marginalized communities are very familiar with the persistence of othering, bullying, and violence in American institutions.[1] From schools to workplaces to places of worship, it seems no place of communal activity in American society is free from the threat of violent words and actions. Higher education is no exception to this.

I am fond of telling my history of higher education students that colleges and universities are both mirrors and sites of origin for cultural movements in the nation's history; therefore, we should not be surprised when the most noble—and most repellent—aspects of our cultural zeitgeist appear on campus. Just as anti-war and civil rights movements were being quelled by militarized police forces in wider society, the same violent suppression was visited on campuses such as Kent State University, and the lesser-known but equally brutal incidents at Jackson State University in Mississippi and South Carolina State University.[2] I share this not to deliver a history lesson (though it is a history that higher education professionals should know), but to make the point that the common perception of higher education institutions not being part of the "real world" is a mistaken presumption.

Instead, students, faculty, staff, and administrators are immersed in contexts where White supremacy, ableism, sexism, homophobia, transphobia, xenophobia, and related vitriolic forms exist as microaggressions, systemic structures, and violence. Failing to understand this is one way that higher education leaders invalidate the existence of those who have experienced these incidents. It also means that those leaders who are most proximal to the communities in the line of fire are betwixt and between advocating structural change and promoting incremental progress while internalizing the criticism of the institutions they are a part of. If this sounds like an untenable position—it is. In previous chapters, I've discussed how cultural taxation and the era of racial reckoning—coupled with a worldwide pandemic—have created an untenable workplace for DEI professionals in this decade.[3] Given this context, why should anyone pursue opportunities to advance equity and inclusion at a higher education institution?

BUILDING CAPACITY AND CAMARADERIE: NEGOTIATING SELF-CARE IN DEI WORK

This is a question I asked new potential colleagues in our diversity education work when I served as assistant vice president for research for the Division of Diversity and Community Engagement at The University of Texas at Austin. In this role, I worked on a team of staff members responsible for presenting interactive workshops to departments and offices across our campus. While our workshops were always voluntary and created in partnership with offices and departments—following the research findings that suggest that mandatory diversity trainings have short-lived results and do little to diminish bias—there were still challenges.[4]

Even with the interest and engagement of leaders in units, it was not uncommon to encounter skeptical team members. Or in the course of a workshop have someone express a view that, while constructed as a question, could reveal unconscious bias invalidating a presenter's identity and/or experience. Comments such as "I'm open to LGBTQ people, but I don't know why I have to agree with their lifestyle" will resonate with diversity educators—a microaggressive statement, one that might be personally painful—but in the role of educator, how does one respond? Is that moment, in fact, a time to respond?

One person having to make these judgments and assessments in real time can be overwhelmed, which is why as a practice we always led workshops as teams. A look of discomfort or a slight pause was our signal to one another: "Can you lead this part of the facilitation? I need a moment to compose myself." We valued the moments of reflection after the workshops, where we were able to note where the facilitation and discussion were particularly strong, or where it seemed the participants disengaged. Importantly, we needed time to restore. As I related to my colleagues, facilitating discussions around issues of identity often impact us on the most personal level; it was not like leading a discussion on physics. We often left these sessions physically and emotionally tired, and knew we needed to find ways to recharge to do the work effectively.

When we realized how interested we were in knowing how a new potential colleague would manage their self-care in leading diversity education workshops, we decided to start a research project from the various vantage points of identity that we held on our team: faculty member, graduate student, postdoctoral fellow, and staff member, in addition to our various intersecting identities as Black, Latina, White, cisgender, queer, male, female, first generation, temporarily able bodied, and working class, to name several of our statuses.

This writing culminated in an article published in the *Journal of Student Affairs Research and Practice*, and it remains one of my favorite collaborative projects. For some of us, it was the first peer-reviewed article we had published—but perhaps most importantly, it demonstrated that our shared experience of intense emotional investment could be understood through the psychological lenses of emotional trauma, racial battle fatigue, and emotional labor.[5]

Our research pointed out a fundamental contradiction in the diversity work performed at predominantly White institutions. The work of educating members of the campus community, which would inspire and motivate institutional change, is incumbent on the efforts of teams such as ours who are often comprised of individuals from historically marginalized identity groups, who grapple with the tensions of resisting and burning out. I was increasingly concerned with a model that placed some of the most marginalized people in universities under the greatest duress—and further disturbed by accounts of professionals leaving the field disillusioned and exhausted. However, two events had me thinking about a new model going forward.

LESSONS FROM ENVIRONMENTALISM: APPLYING PRINCIPLES OF SUSTAINABILITY TO EQUITY WORK

One of the most admirable aspects of the students I have taught in the past few years is their focus on environmental justice. They often use the term *sustainability*, which the United Nations' Brundtland Commission defines as "meeting the needs of the present without compromising the ability of future generations to meet their own needs."[6] While usually framed in terms of economic development and environmental protection, this concept maps well onto doing equity and inclusion work. A generation ago, when I started working on diversity initiatives and simultaneously researching best practices as a member of the Harvard National Campus Diversity Project, we frequently worked with and studied faculty, staff, and students who were stretched to their absolute limit, making incremental progress, and always cognizant of what we called the "hit by a bus" principle—if that key administrator, student leader, or faculty member resigned, took a new job, graduated, or God forbid, got hit by a bus . . . who would continue their work? Quite often, we learned there was nobody waiting in the wings.

A sustainable, restorative approach to diversity, equity, inclusion, and belonging work would mean that individuals would be able to engage in their efforts in a way that permitted growth and deep commitment, but also provided ways to step away from the intensity of the work—supported by peers and institutional mechanisms. The work would therefore be restorative rather than subtractive, and sustainable—careers could advance while bodies and minds could heal and grow in a healthy way. As I pondered this idea, I tried to find the appropriate metaphor or comparison to bring this concept forward. The inspiration, it seemed, was literally right in front of my face.

GETTING FIT IN THE EQUITY GYM

I was never much of an athlete and have historically devoted little time to thinking about my physical health. However, advancing age and a family history of diabetes brought me to a realization that I needed to get serious about physical fitness. My realization came with a sense of dread—the process of getting fit can be very intimidating and overwhelming, with confusing jargon and conflicting advice (not to mention those folks who are very fit and comfortable in the gym). I found, however, that what worked for me was a program called Get FIT for faculty and staff at UT Austin.

Described as an "11-week fitness, weight loss and behavior change program," and run by the Fitness Institute of Texas, "the goal of Get FIT is to help participants improve their fitness, lose body fat and implement health behavior changes that can be maintained for a lifetime."[7] As great as the workout sessions are, what makes Get FIT work is the peer experience. You get to know your fellow Get FITters, some of whom you probably know from your work on campus. There is a sense of accountability, as you start noticing when a friend is absent. You also find other aspects of fitness to involve yourself in, such as the dietitian seminars and weekend walks. In short, it's a workout ecosystem that welcomes the most dedicated gym rat and the most exercise-averse person alike.

I was working with a community-based educational organization that wanted to push their equity commitments further than they had in the past, and we decided the best way to do this was to partner with them over a year with episodic check-ins. The "one and done" workshops were ultimately unsatisfying, but this longitudinal engagement gave us time to build a relationship and trust. Further, we could assess how their equity work was going over time. I referred to our work as an "equity workout."

The analogy is quite sound. Getting fit, like becoming committed to an anti-racist, anti-bias practice, usually means a change of mindset and significant effort. However, getting started on the work can be intimidating. Like working out, initially engaging with diversity, equity, and inclusion can seem to result in very modest results, if any at all. Being around people with similar goals is motivating, and they provide support particularly when you might feel less motivated. A good trainer will push you to do more than you think you can, but not to the extent that you injure yourself . . . and they will not allow you to "coast." Similarly, working with a "DEI coach" who recommends ways in which to further immerse yourself in anti-racism, anti-bias experiences can be incredibly motivating.

Just as "the balance is 80% diet and 20% exercise," one's "diet" of media, information, culture, and social settings also facilitates a sustainable orientation toward equity and inclusion.[8] One's choice of entertainment, literature, and news complements the intentional efforts from engagement, dialogue, and action. Surrounding oneself with friends and colleagues who support the efforts sets in motion the mindset and milieu conducive to a sustainable environment for anti-racist, anti-bias practice.

Restorative and sustainable equity and social justice practice also demand humility and the state of mind of a constant learner. Invariably, there will be aspects of the journey that are difficult, where the process of learning may be somewhat painful and require significant self-reflection. Discovering our own unexamined biases and how they might limit our equity and inclusion work can be at times difficult, awkward, and downright cringeworthy. The temptation to look outward rather than inward is a continual struggle. However, for the reflective equity advocate in a reflective, restorative, and sustainable practice, "becoming aware of their own beliefs, biases, and values, understanding how such beliefs impact their ability to effectively engage with all people, and approaching all individuals and situations with openness and humility" is the goal.[9]

One of our Bravely Confronting Racism faculty members and the former president of Huston-Tillotson University (Austin's first university and historically Black university), Dr. Colette Pierce Burnette reminds us that while some social conventions may proclaim the importance of being "race blind," what we actually need is for more of us to be "race brave."[10] I'm often asked, "What do I do if I make a mistake in generalizing about a population?" or "What if I use a wrong or outdated term in referring to people of a certain identity?"

My answer is, "You're human. You likely will."

Even when one has a finely tuned equity lens and keeps current with the literature, there are gray areas and spaces where there is variance and no consensus regarding terminology and labels. When that happens, however, the focus should be on our own accountability: apologizing and ensuring that whatever harm we inflicted (intentionally or otherwise) is acknowledged, and working to rebuild relationships that may have been damaged, rather than focusing solely on our own discomfort.[11] We follow many of the principles associated with restorative justice as we work to repair the harm we might have caused.[12]

This is when the communities we have so carefully and purposefully built come to our aid—helping us recover from the stumbles we will invariably make, and providing the appropriate support, pushback, and reflection that makes our work meaningful and impactful. Educational researcher Dr. Sonia Nieto, one of my role models and a pioneering multicultural educator, explains how circles of critical friends impact and advance our equity work. While Dr. Nieto's definition is centered on the work of K–12 teachers, it is very applicable to our community of DEI-focused scholar-practitioners, as well.

> It is imperative that future teachers learn to become critical colleagues, that is, teachers who are capable of developing respectful but critical relationships with their peers. Working in isolation, no teacher can single-handedly effect the changes that are needed in an entire school, at least not in the long term. Developing a community of critical friends opens up teachers' classrooms and their perspectives, so that they can acknowledge that all students should be the concern of all teachers. What is needed are not simply peers who support one another, essential as this may be, but also peers who debate, critique, and challenge one another to go beyond their current ideas and practices.[13]

I often encourage colleagues to think about our equity work in terms of *brave* spaces versus the commonly appropriated *safe* space. Safety, in this regard, is an illusory and impossible assurance, as the NASPA Research and Policy Institute found that "safe space is never actually safe." Instead, "the concept of a brave space encompasses all of what the sectors discussed in this work regard as safe spaces, but clarifies that these environments are challenging and that students are expected to participate within them."[14] Bravery connotes the necessity of support equal to adversarial positions and dissonance. We are not guaranteed safety, as learning and growing often initially feels risky and uncertain, but as Dr. Nieto describes, a circle of peers committed to navigating these experiences in collaboration can help foster the best version of ourselves as a commitment to serving our community in an equitable manner.

CENTERING COMMUNITY BUILDING IN SUSTAINABLE AND RESTORATIVE RESISTANCE

In my academic work, consulting, and professional development experience as faculty and cochair of the Institute for Educational Management (IEM) and Bravely Confronting Racism (BCR) at Harvard, I have often interacted with DEI faculty and administrators who have both the passion and motivation to engage deeply on efforts to transform their institutional spaces. Convenings such as these are essential, because not everybody is in a professional space with supportive peers immediately proximal to their work. These colloquies are significant for restoring resistance capital, which is an important aspect of sustaining diversity, equity, and inclusion work.

Years ago, I was in an IEM session led by one of my heroes in the field, former university president Dr. Beverly Daniel Tatum. As Dr. Tatum closed out her session, drawing on years of psychological research relating to diminishing prejudice and bias, a participant asked a question: By virtue of the fact that everyone in the room made the professional, time, and economic investment to be in this space, wasn't this in fact an exemplar of "preaching to the choir"—assembling the interested and potentially not expanding the potential impact of the work? Without missing a beat, Dr. Tatum replied, "Sometimes, the choir needs practice."

In other words, to sustain equity and inclusion movements, it is critically important to build community. Networking and learning from colleagues across the nation and the world, as well as creating connections that can be enduring beyond these institutional settings, is as foundational as expanding the reach of DEI efforts in our particular circumstances. What my cochair Dr. Robbin Chapman and I endeavor to create in our institute are the conditions to continue the conversation well beyond the weeks our participants spend in Bravely Confronting Racism. The pandemic ushered in a rapid learning mode for using distance technology; miles and time zones can be spanned through these technologies and apps. It is increasingly possible to facilitate communities of reflection and practice with participants in Galway, Ireland, Ottawa, Canada, and Minneapolis, Minnesota (factoring in time differences, of course).

BEFORE YOU SIGN: OPTIMAL CONDITIONS FOR TAKING ON DEI-FOCUSED ROLES

Even with the creation of restorative and sustaining communities of scholar-practitioners, we still hear our colleagues despair because they are in institutional spaces that have not embraced and prioritized equity and inclusion strategies. What, then, if you are one of the few people working in these roles at your college or university? This goes back to one of my core principles when I advise people interested in taking on DEI positions: don't be the only person working on DEI in the unit, division, college, or university. When considering opportunities, knowing how diversity, equity, and inclusion is articulated and enacted through strategic planning, the institutional mission, and the actions and words of leadership is essential. *This does not mean that plans, actions, and rhetoric have to be perfect.* A key question to ask is: Who will be doing the work with me? Who are my potential allies and coconspirators? If the answers to these questions are lacking, please proceed with caution. You may be taking on a disproportionate amount of responsibility and agency for enacting change, and you might be doing it alone—hardly a sustainable path going forward.

Many of us doing the work of advancing equity at PWIs represent historically marginalized identities. This creates a tension, particularly if the "bench strength" on equity and inclusion is shallow or nonexistent. Race and cultural studies scholar Dr. Sara Ahmed encapsulates this concern when she relates her experience in an administrative appointment:

> I began to attend faculty meetings. I was the only person of color at these meetings. It is important to note that I noticed this: whiteness tends to be visible to those who do not inhabit it (though not

> always, and not only). During the discussion of one item at a faculty meeting on equality, the dean said something like "race is too difficult to deal with." I remember wanting to challenge this. But the difficulty of speaking about racism as a person of color meant that I did not speak up during but after the meeting, and even then I wrote rather than spoke. Saying that race is "too difficult" is how racism gets reproduced, I put in an email to the dean. The belief that racism is inevitable is how racism becomes inevitable, I pointed out.[15]

This vignette features all the hazards of being the sole bearer of equity and inclusion. The diminution of race, or citing it as irrelevant or too complex to engage with, leaves those members of the community who live with the daily social consequences of race with a sense of erasure and exclusion. As Ahmed relates, when such comments are made, the DEI scholar-practitioner must calculate *when* and *how* to intervene. There is the danger of, on one hand becoming a passive participant in enabling inequity, and on the other assuming the role of the "diversity cop," ready to engage the countless microaggressions that emerge in each meeting and interaction. Both roles are unappealing and untenable.

I find that "pregaming" meeting dynamics can be one strategy for responding to these experiences. Conferencing with members of the team and seeking their input about how to intervene or disrupt deficit-oriented discourse in meetings does two things: first, it makes the team aware that these dynamics are at play, and second, it distributes the responsibility for addressing them to everyone—not just to one person. Further unpacking the power dynamics—race, gender, seniority, and organizational status—can illuminate patterns in groups that are seemingly invisible to those who benefit from them. Who gets the first word and last word on a topic? Do some voices end conversation while others invite greater engagement and conversation? These patterns may be well established and hard to notice for those who have been in the network for some time; the benefit of new people entering these spaces is that it is an opportunity to reflect on prior practice. Along with pregaming meeting dynamics, there is a need to reflect and assess the impact on meetings—in the meetings themselves, by interviewing team members, and even via anonymous survey, depending on the size of the group.

OBSERVATIONS FROM THE FIELD: EQUITY IS A PRIORITY

Over the years as a convener of higher education leaders in the research and professional development realm, I have found that more and more of the challenges that face administrators and other leaders are linked to equity and inclusion. The fact that CIOs and CFOs, as well as provosts and deans, frequently find themselves working through dilemmas seemingly far afield from their functional areas—combined with the realities of a nation and world racked with the aftereffects of a pandemic and racial inequality—means that even leaders who assiduously avoided "controversial" issues centered on diversity, equity, inclusion, and belonging are having to engage. More than ever, knowledge and experience related to equity and inclusion are core competencies for leadership, much like familiarity with budgeting and human resources is expected in these roles.

Articulating Equity Through Diversity Statements

As a result, many institutions are enabling search committees to require statements explaining a candidate's commitment to and investment in diversity and inclusion. The need for the "diversity statement" speaks to the fact that DEI concerns are commonly perceived as peripheral to one's teaching and research, or as an "add-on" to administrative prowess, "rather than something at the very core" of one's research and practice.[16] Negotiating this reality is why I believe that statements are instructive in understanding how members of our institution value and advance equity broadly, regardless of academic and/or professional expertise and interest—although in my own process, I look for a candidate's commitment to anti-racism and anti-bias in all materials. Unsurprisingly, there is some controversy associated with diversity statements. Some argue that the statements serve as a litmus test for a political leaning, or that they are a violation of academic freedom.[17] However, if we think of engagement in diversity, equity, and inclusion efforts as a necessary competency for those who work in colleges and universities, much like excellence in teaching, diversity statements become a sensible way to ascertain how candidates understand representation and inclusion in the institutional context, and as importantly, what they might bring to our institution regarding their values and commitment to underrepresented communities.

My UT Austin colleague Dr. Charlotte Canning and I were concerned about the swell of voices that opposed diversity statements. These arguments typically originated from a view that hiring practices innately come from a stance of objectivity, which as scholars and researchers in social sciences as well as people from historically marginalized communities we can attest is simply inaccurate. Implicit biases about institutional prestige, for instance, are rampant in our profession: as my professor Dr. Richard Chait would often say, "Nobody is agnostic about Harvard." Ascribing higher value—or scrutiny—to institutions, both ones we know by reputation and those we do not, is commonplace, to name one form of alleged objectivity that does not in practice exist.

The premise that not one demographic, identity group, or job function has more or less responsibility for advancing our institutional values is exemplified through hearing how all members contribute to creating a more welcoming institutional environment, and diminishes the cultural taxation that underrepresented faculty, staff, and administration frequently experience.[18] Contrary to the assumption that there is an expected outcome and orthodoxy in such statements, Charlotte and I instead argued for a diversity of diversity statements:

> To be sure, requiring such statements runs the risk of participating in what Roderick Ferguson calls the "bureaucratization of

> diversity"—institutional lip service that does not actually bring about change. In order for diversity statements to avoid this pitfall, they must ask faculty members not to toe a line or embrace a single ideology but to demonstrate deep engagement with their students and their community. *There can be no single model for this* [emphasis added], because what constitutes diversity, equity, and inclusion in the rehearsal room, science lab, playing field, library, lecture hall, or seminar room will differ by discipline and instructor.[19]

Statements can advance intentionality to action and accountability in a broad manner, allowing each member to express their achievements and aspirations in expanding access and inclusion from a multiplicity of vantage points. The DEI scholar-practitioner has a diverse constituency of colleagues to collaborate and partner with in their work.

TAKING ON THE CHALLENGE: DEI-TEMPERED RADICALS IN THE IVORY TOWER

Even with fruitful connections to colleagues near and far, a restorative practice of embracing equity and inclusion, committing to the equity workout replete with the right "diet," an understanding of the institutional commitments to equity and inclusion, pregaming meeting dynamics for inclusive outcomes, and embracing statements to build teams with equity mindsets, advancing and sustaining DEI work can still be challenging. In our research on Black faculty working in predominantly White institutional contexts, we have found Meyerson's tempered radical framework to be a useful conceptualization of how these individuals enact sustainable, restorative lives of resistance. Meyerson terms tempered radicals as "informal leader[s] who quietly challenge prevailing wisdom and provokes cultural transformation."[20]

Meyerson establishes that while tempered radicals can often disagree with institutional actions, they have decided to stay in the organization over leaving, employing a strategy of quietly working to incite change while working within the institution. A similar framing comes from Kezar and colleagues' "tempered grassroots leadership," where this work does not compromise their values or identities for the sake of "fitting in"—they are leaders who are "less visible, less coordinated, and less vested with formal authority . . . more local, more diffuse, more opportunistic, and more humble than the activity attributed to the modern-day hero."[21]

The tempered radical conceptualization is comprised of five techniques: (a) disruptive self-expression, (b) verbal jujitsu, (c) broadening impact through negotiation, (d) leveraging small wins, and (e) strategic alliance building. The first tactic, disruptive self-expression, occurs when a tempered radical proclaims resistance in small ways—via the expression of identity and values through dress, scheduling, office decor, leadership behaviors, and language. The second strategy, verbal jujitsu, entails turning personal threats into opportunities by redirecting or obliquely challenging negative statements, thus creating opportunities for positive change.[22]

The third tactic entails broadening impact through negotiation. This requires seeking the broader issues to which localized encounters are attached. Fourth, tempered radicals leverage small wins, which requires blurring the lines of organizational culture and language; this technique highlights the importance of appropriately framing the meaning of small wins. The final mechanism by which radicals create change is strategic alliance building, which includes organizing a response to a shared threat or opportunity, or organizing for personal and professional support. This technique develops a collective framing of an issue among diverse stakeholders through either formal or informal group mechanisms. The tolls of tempered radicalism can be steep psychologically and emotionally, depending on the degree to which the radicalism is enacted. Despite myriad challenges, tempered radicals tend to persist, working quietly to incite change in their environments.[23]

Our research extended Meyerson's framework for Black faculty, as we learned that *authenticity* pertained to their scholarly and professional endeavors as well as their establishing roots in the surrounding community beyond the institution, and anchoring their work through the support and nurturing of students.[24] Years later, I look at this study and realize that the symbiotic relationship between students and faculty can be extended to administrators and staff. I also think the relationships are far more nuanced in the post-George Floyd era—a tension between immediate and radical change and the cautious, sometimes plodding pace of change in higher education. Yet there are synergies and convergences in institutional direction and student activism that are essential to capitalize upon. Most evident, in my reckoning, is the threat to academic freedom and inclusion in states instituting bans on books and how history is taught. The response from higher education must transcend discrete constituencies—faculty, administration, staff, and students—and advance a common understanding that colleges and universities regress and wither when governmental policy dictates what is taught.

ENDURING ALLIANCES: LONG-TERM PARTNERSHIPS AND AFFILIATIONS

If there is a consistent thread in the two-and-a-half decades I have spent working as an administrator and scholar focused on equity and inclusion, it would be the enduring partnerships and mentoring that have transcended roles and distance. I feel fortunate that my research and practice has come together in such a way that many of the authors of the concepts and findings that have guided the best practices in creating supportive campus climates are people I have had the opportunity to know, and even at times collaborate with. I think it speaks to the kinds of people who dedicate their lives and careers to improving the experiences of all participants in higher education—particularly those who are most marginalized and excluded. Motivated by a sense of justice and integrity, I suspect that when we found each other—"fellow travelers," if you will—a bond was forged. Additionally, many of us operated in similar scholarly and social circles, a six degrees of DEI separation, so to speak.

I was fortunate to be immersed as an emerging scholar in several nurturing communities. As a Spencer Foundation predoctoral fellow, I had exposure to convenings with some of the foremost thinkers in the diversity area. At the same time, some of the opportunities were overwhelming, and I navigated feelings of inadequacy and impostor syndrome.[25] Once, I arrived at a conference reception, walked into the room, and feeling overwhelmed, walked immediately out. As I left the venue, I must have had a look of shock on my face because another scholar stopped me and asked if I had met anyone in the space. I stammered that I had not, and the scholar offered to introduce me to people he knew in the space. I ended up staying at the reception and making connections—great training for a young doctoral student. I'm eternally grateful for running into Dr. James Earl Davis many years ago, and he continues to be a mentor and support to the present day.

While our disciplinary and professional trajectories will necessarily mean that the societies and affiliations will differ, I share this vignette to show how these engagements can be spaces of nurturing and support. I am similarly intrigued by how the tendrils of networks reach through different disciplines, institutions, regions, and nations. And of course, through organizations such as the Institute for Educational Management and Bravely Confronting Racism, we are creating more convenings that lay the foundation for lasting partnerships beyond the brief time that these meetings typically last. For DEI-focused scholar-practitioners, I emphatically proclaim "find your people!" These can be organizations expressly focused on DEI or divisions within larger societies. However these spaces are configured, it's essential to establish a foothold in those arenas. I feel replenished after spending time with coconspirators across the nation and world even if only for a day or two annually.

WHEN IT'S ALL TOO MUCH

Throughout this chapter, I have presented strategies to help DEI scholar-practitioners navigate seemingly untenable roles during an unprecedented time. The level of societal polarization coupled with the seismic impact of pandemics, mass shootings, war, and political strife, means that the decade of the 2020s resembles other watershed years: 1968 comes to mind, as many journalists and scholars have considered.[26] While the verdict is out regarding whether the past few years will rank among those that shattered America, it is unreservedly a historically tumultuous and emotionally draining era that we are presently living through.[27] Among others, higher education scholar Dr. Kevin McClure has tracked the declining levels of morale and increasing levels of turnover that have been deemed "The Great Resignation." However, he sees this as a peak in a twenty-year epoch of burnout, low pay, and incessant stress.[28] This moment, then, is more of a tipping point than touch paper. Regardless, I have both witnessed and advised an unprecedented number of higher education professionals concerning leaving the field in the past several years.

Until recently in my career as a scholar and student affairs professional, I have been resolute in advising colleagues and mentees that their informed professional perspectives are needed and doing what I can to convince talented scholar-practitioners to stay in the field. But as I've been in community with more of my colleagues—particularly women of color, and particularly Black women—my advice has become far more nuanced and introspective.

Centering Our Well-Being: Acknowledging the Existence of John(etta) Henryism

Inspired by these discussions on belonging, professional journeys, and the decision forks we face, I wrote an essay for *Fortune* soon after George Floyd's murder, framing the stressors on Black professionals in the workplace through social epidemiologist Dr. Sherman James's phenomenon of "John Henryism" (also termed "Johnetta Henryism").[29] While James's research observed psychological and physiological problems including heart disease and hypertension among working-class Black men, I extended this to the experiences of white-collar Black professionals often exhorted to be "twice as good, to go half as far," as Michelle Obama wrote in *Becoming*.[30]

To address this, I appealed to workplaces to ensure that anti-racist work is not placed solely on the backs of Black professionals; certifying that workplaces promote mentally and physically healthy lifestyles for all—while simultaneously noting the unique stressors for employees who are Black, indigenous, or people of color, particularly during a time of racial reckoning; and creating and supporting resource groups for community and collaboration, having unbiased rubrics for promotion, and professionalizing the uncompensated labor of BIPOC team members through compensation and time releases.[31]

The response from this opinion piece was significant, both from media outlets and social media. Perhaps the most affirming response I received came from Dr. James himself, who kindly sent a note: "It's a terrific essay. I also read the hyperlinks to other articles included in your piece, and in addition, viewed your videotaped presentation on "cultural taxation."[32] I've already shared your essay with several former PhD students (African American) of mine who, as junior faculty at major research universities, are trying to survive "cultural taxation" at their universities. Your ideas will prove invaluable." As someone who perceives himself as an "perpetually emerging scholar," there is nothing more validating than having those scholars whose work in which you situate your own say, "Well done."

It was also wonderful to learn that Dr. James will be writing a book on John Henryism, and that perhaps this essay introduced the concept to a broader audience—I certainly heard this from emails I'd received from colleagues: "I'd never heard of John Henryism, but as soon as I read it, that's exactly right." Researching and writing about John Henryism further emphasized that Black and other people of color were paying the price of advancing equity and inclusion with their health, and even their lives, in a variety of fields (including higher education).

Mentoring, Vulnerability, and Resisting: Reckoning with the Realities of Higher Education as a Profession

This shift was additionally informed by my decade-long participation as moderator of a panel on mentoring with a cohort of some of the wisest scholars I have had the opportunity to know: Drs. Darren Ranco (University of Maine, Orono), Duchess Harris (Macalester College), Herman Beavers (University of Pennsylvania), David Cort (University of Massachusetts at Amherst), and Butch Ware (University of California, Santa Barbara). Though it's a panel, it quickly shifts into an extended dialogue with classes of Career Enhancement Fellows from the Institute for Citizens and Scholars, where mentees and mentors can express their vulnerability and delve deeply into questions about identity, scholarship, and lifestyle.

I consider this to be one of the most remarkable convenings in higher education—dozens of scholars, from a wide range of disciplines and institutional types, bonded by their potential for excellence in their respective fields and being members of historically underrepresented identities in the academy. Demographically, and vibe-wise, it is unlike virtually any space I inhabit in academia: it is a convening where the humanity and totality of scholars is paramount. Discussions about impact factors and h-indices dissipate as family, balance, and self-actualization become the prominent discourse.

When we talk about mentoring, I hear my colleagues' vulnerability and their urging of emerging scholars to resist the academy's desire to shape them into roles that mute their very being. Particularly resonant in my memory is Butch reminding all of us—mentees, mentors, panelists, and administrators—that we are the authors of our life story, and too many of us are writing the story with broken tools. The Career Enhancement Fellowship year is a structured space for restoration and sustainability, a refuge from a career pathway that too often infringes on our well-being and mental health. Much of this book presents how scholar-practitioners can resist these pressures, but as I consider all I've learned in higher education, no resistance seems worth our souls. Yet, our profession can be unrelenting in its demands for our time and energy.

Too often, withdrawing, regrouping, and even retreating is seen as surrender rather than the ultimate form of resistance. Finding alternative ways to impact policy, research, and practice, or even abandoning the work for a time allows us to live and even extend our lives. When I worked with my friend and colleague psychologist Dr. Aaron Rochlen and a team of our graduate students on a study regarding fathers who were striving to balance their familial roles with their pursuit of tenure in the professoriate, it struck me how much of a sacrifice higher education exacts from those working in the field:

> Lionel stated that there was always more work to be done: the job "never says you've done enough." Mattias further emphasized this concern: "The workday never finishes. I do a lot of work at home in the evening. Computers have made things much more complicated . . . not only do you have to be reading and trying to get writing done, but there is a constant stream of e-mails that you need to deal with." Steve shared this perspective, saying: "It took a toll on my marriage. My wife was really upset with how little time I had for us. She would say, 'I don't want to live like this.'"[33]

These comments were torturous for us to hear, but they landed very close to home for me. After all, at the time I was also a new father, untenured, and uncertain whether I would meet the bar for promotion. The study, in many ways, was conceived to give me (and our research team of aspiring scholars) a sense of "life on the other side." (Rochlen was already tenured, so we assumed he knew!)

Ironically, this publication captured the interest of the media and brought our research to another level of prominence, potentially moving me closer to tenure three years later. However, the words of our participants in this study stayed with me. I can't pretend to be a model of work-life balance, but I have become very responsive to when I am out of equilibrium. More accurately, the people in my life that matter most bring it to my attention, and I am grateful that they have patience with me as I stumble to find the appropriate measure of all my life roles: dad, husband, son, friend, mentor, administrator, scholar, and hobbyist.

I believe it's a worthwhile exercise to ask ourselves "Is it worth it?" and not be afraid to answer honestly. This question can help us prioritize, minimize, or eliminate aspects of what we do to answer the question affirmatively. We can also assign time windows to our goals: "I am interested in pursuing this opportunity for three more years; at that time, I will then look for an advancement of responsibilities and compensation." Or perhaps you want to be more present as a parent, partner, or friend, which will necessitate a change in how you work. Whatever the rationale, it is valid and essential to consider your own agency in shaping your trajectory. With this mindset, sometimes the option of exiting (echoing Albert Hirschman's exit, voice, or loyalty model) is the most appropriate choice, rather than voice (vocalizing opposition to provoke change) or loyalty (investing time in the organization in the hopes that change will come).[34]

SUGGESTIONS FROM THE SPORTING STAGE: PUTTING OUR HEALTH FIRST

The power of exiting, saying "no" to the work you love and excel at, to preserve yourself, was exemplified at the 2020 Olympics by the legendary gymnast Simone Biles. After enrapturing the world with her performance in the 2016 Olympics, Biles soon became arguably the GOAT—"greatest of all time"—in the field of competitive gymnastics, with twenty-five world championship medals, more than any gymnast in history.[35] Certainly, I would challenge anyone to watch Biles's reality-defying triple-double at the 2019 FIG Artistic Gymnastics World Championships and not walk away questioning whether gravity actually exists.[36] At the peak of her career, with the expectation of sweeping the 2020–21 Olympics, Simone Biles shocked the world by pulling out of the competition.[37]

While the shortsighted pundit class contributed acerbic and thoughtless takes on Biles's decision, more insight into her situation explained many of the stressors she was negotiating. In September 2021, Biles testified to the US Senate details of her abuse at the hands of US Gymnastics Olympic doctor, Larry Nassar, who was sentenced to 175 years in prison in 2018 after sexually assaulting hundreds of young women, many of whom were minors.[38] Empathically, we all must feel a scintilla of the horror, stress, and disempowerment that Biles felt at this moment, and likely still feels. I am still in awe of Biles's strength of character and resolute decision to put her own well-being and mental health at the forefront and *not* compete—as a ravenous, sport-obsessed public demanded that she prioritize their needs and desires above her own well-being.[39]

HATERS GONNA HATE: NAVIGATING MISOGYNOIR AND ASSOCIATED HYPERSCRUTINY

Indeed, many commentators who labeled her decision as "selfish" and "sociopathic" had me recalling Maya Angelou's age-old wisdom: "When someone shows you who they are, believe them."[40] It was not lost on me that the most vitriolic responses came from fairly mediocre White men, who seemed to believe that dignity is only afforded to Black women who are compliant and submissive.[41] This unhinged backlash was a textbook example of what communications scholar Dr. Moya Bailey has termed "misogynoir," anti-Black and misogynistic representations that permeate and influence images and perceptions of Black women, especially in cultural and digital spaces such as social media.[42] In my own experience, these indignities and affronts happen frequently in the ivory tower.

Biles's decision is instructive regarding how we think about our own careers. If Biles (as well as Naomi Osaka, a tennis superstar who similarly withdrew from Wimbledon in 2021) can prioritize her life over her work at the highest level, surely her courage can inform our own.[43] Most of us in institutions of higher education aren't doing our work under such high levels of public scrutiny, but we have likely experienced some of the blowback and criticism these two Black women have. Biles and Osaka illustrate to us that there is another way of addressing the unyielding pressure in our roles: to step away from the work in favor of our well-being. As someone who has long called for a greater focus on the mental health of our students, I believe it's high time that we bring that same concern to our own well-being: "Physical and mental stressors contribute to the maelstrom of issues confronting the 21st-century Black academic. The emerging body of literature on Black academics has presented institutions with the reality that this population leads radically different lives compared with White faculty; yet, the acknowledgment of these differences has been slow and not reflected in institutional values."[44]

The decisions we make are incredibly personal and are contingent on our individual tolerances and expectations in our roles, institutional contexts, and lives. But I hope I can be one who reminds all of us in the DEI space, "I am the master of my fate, I am the captain of my soul."[45] As all-encompassing as our institutional and individual challenges are, none of us should sacrifice our well-being to rectify them. We can take a break—the challenges will likely be there if we choose to return.

Conclusion

HOW DO YOU CLOSE a conversation that needs to continue? That's the challenge I'm tasked with. In the prior pages, I think we've just scratched the surface regarding the critical discussions we must have in our institutional spaces, between colleagues, with students, and in our broader community. Daring to disrupt inequitable structures is courageous work, and I thank you for engaging, regardless of where you might be on your journey toward inclusive wellness.

The importance of courage can't be overstated. In a recent conversation with my dear friend and colleague Dr. Robbin Chapman, we lamented how many potential allies and coconspirators in the fight for equity and inclusion essentially surrender out of fear. Fear of saying the wrong thing. Fear of being viewed as a "radical." Fear of losing the support of supposed friends who expected them to not rock the boat. The resistance we've discussed is not possible if there's no restoration—not just from the perspective of those directly engaged in doing the work, but from colleagues, coworkers, and family members who may be some degrees of separation from the front line. In the words of Dr. Marybeth Gasman and Ufuoma Abiola, "White faculty need to step up."[1] Our work of achieving campus environments that embrace diversity, equity, inclusion, and belonging must be equitably distributed.

The stakes could not be higher. As I write this, five years have passed since the White supremacist rally in Charlottesville, Virginia—home to a prestigious university—sparked by that community's decision to remove

Confederate statues.[2] Minimizing the real threat that exists from racism and anti-Semitism can metastasize into violence; our institutions should be the bulwark from authoritarianism. As my friend, colleague, and Presidential Medal of Freedom recipient Dr. Juliet V. Garcia has said, our universities must "nurture, defend, and sustain the democracy of the United States."[3] I can think of no more essential work toward this goal than ensuring that our institutions are welcoming and inclusive to all members of our community.

When I discussed the privilege payoff in chapter 4, I explicitly recommended that the conversations on equity and inclusion take place with White people. I recently watched *The Problem with Jon Stewart*, a new series featuring the former *Daily Show* host. In this episode, Stewart attempted just this—a discussion about structural inequity and racism with three White people. Stewart was joined by La Salle University sociology professor Dr. Charles "Chip" Gallagher, Lisa Bond of Race2Dinner (a collective that facilitates discussions on race over, you guessed it, dinner), and political commentator Andrew Sullivan.[4] It was telling that Stewart, Gallagher, and Bond had "done the work"—reading and reasoning about the third rail in American discourse, race. Sullivan, however, entered the discussion from a Horatio Alger framing, dismissing the structural and historical issues that have led to economic, political, and judicial inequalities. In fact, Sullivan engaged in what I call *inequity denialism*—using essentialized data points and weaving in deficit narratives about communities of color to explain away disparities and camouflage social advantages and disadvantages distributed by race and ethnicity. Frustration mounted, tempers flared, and the segment ended unceremoniously. To quote Stewart, "It . . . did . . . not . . . go . . . well."[5]

Upon reflection, though, I found some praiseworthy aspects of the discussion. First, no people of color had to play the role of educator, mediator, or soother of hurt feelings. Midway through the discussion, Stewart attempted to find middle ground and connection between the panelists. And on some level, each of the panelists exhibited courage by remaining in the conversation (I truly thought that at least one of the panelists would storm off). My colleagues in DEI education generally agree that one shared agreement in discussions must be "don't expect closure," and with this discussion that was the case. I wondered what a follow-up discussion would have looked like: Would Sullivan, who did acknowledge the role of redlining in creating patterns of racial inequity in housing and wealth distribution, be open to the concept of opportunity hoarding, where those who are in positions of societal privilege gatekeep and zealously guard access to networks and opportunity, which has the result of pushing out those who are on the periphery or further down the socioeconomic quintiles?[6] Back to our analogy of the equity workout, It seems that this particular journey was just getting started, and a group of peers committed to critical reflection and support might have advanced and illuminated some of the thinking in the discussion.

Similarly, the sustainability of our work is a paramount concern and a thread I've pulled on through this book. Words like "exhaustion" and "burden" are peppered throughout the prior chapters, so ensuring that the essential work of diversity, equity, inclusion, and belonging is supported and not draining to those most engaged on these issues. Restorative and sustaining practices—centering one's well-being, distributing responsibility and accountability for advancing equity, and challenging and dismantling discriminatory, unjust structures—will be the only way the work progresses and moves from the shoulders of an invested few to a commitment that meets our institutional aspirations on the axes of morality, policy, economics, and human capital. Our institutions, by mottoes and mission statements, frequently talk the talk, but do we walk the walk?

In the spirit of restoration and sustainability, I want to close with a reminder very similar to the one we've frequently heard—"You are what you consume."[7] I hope this book encourages you to explore the works I cite here—some are scholarly, some are mass media, and some are audiovisual media. The concepts you sit with and mull over will excite and challenge you, and become part of your sustainable practice. I also think this should be fun. There's nothing I enjoy better than the mash-up of social commentary with humor, which is why I find programs like W. Kamau Bell's *United Shades of America*, John Oliver's *Last Week Tonight*, and Robin Thede's *A Black Lady Sketch Show*, to name a few, excellent examples of comedy intertwined with analysis of social inequity and inclusion. Finding programs, podcasts, articles, and books that explore DEI topics is a great pastime, and sharing those findings with your community can be a bonding experience.

At the same time, I think it's important to be aware of how the recalcitrant forces to inclusion frame their arguments. A few years ago, the *New York Times* columnist Frank Bruni visited UT Austin and spoke with our students about his concerns about how social media and AI are curating gardens of information sources based on what we like—creating silos of thought and reinforcing much of what we already believe. I think this analysis is half correct: there is a need for us to find community and those who experience the world similarly to us; I'm reminded of a conversation with scholar of trans* studies Dr. Z Nicolazzo about how trans* youth create and discover communities of support via social media, which is incredibly empowering and literally a lifeline for many young people who have persistent feelings of being alone and "the only one."[8] Historically marginalized community members can use social media for organizing and finding resources, which strengthens movements.

On the other hand, some of the most rewarding learning experiences I have had are those in which I have met and built a relationship with someone whose experiences and worldview differ significantly from mine; these relationships took time (and courage) to develop, and we had to prioritize respect and agreeing to disagree. Often, we would bond over things we had in common—family, food, music—which built the foundation for the more difficult points of engagement. We might chat about a news event or an op-ed we both read and try to understand how we each framed the issue—and what was hidden or assumed in the accounts we had read.

I experience this same back and forth when I listen to *Intelligence Squared* podcasts, which are modeled after the Cambridge Union debates; indeed, I often direct students to watch the 1965 debate between James Baldwin and William Buckley to appreciate the importance of reasoned discourse.[9]

I suspect that debates, while important, aren't solely what most of us are seeking on our journeys to DEI practice. Empathy and understanding are essential parts of our drive for understanding (which I often phrase as "understanding *how* someone comes to a worldview, rather than understanding *why* they have a certain worldview"). This comes down to those human interactions, one-on-one, in small groups, requisite with awkwardness, uncomfortable moments, and yes, moments of bonding and breakthroughs. I again return to courage—courage to broach difficult conversations, courage to be wrong, courage to return to a dialogue when we stumble or are incorrect, and courage to keep doing it.

The analogy I would proffer goes back to my experience teaching my daughter to roller skate (a lost art among the younger generation). After several exhausting sessions, it appeared that Katherine was still shuffling and moving very slowly and cautiously. It didn't look like much fun, and frankly, it looked as if she was on the verge of panic.

I asked, "Katherine, are you afraid of falling?" She responded, "Yes." I thought for a minute about what I had learned as a novice skater and then said, "You know what? Falling is part of skating. You can't skate with confidence if you're afraid to fall. Let's find a way to fall so you won't hurt yourself, and I'll bet you'll be skating like a pro soon."

That was the key.

Knowing that falling is inevitable, and how to fall to minimize injury, made Katherine the confident skater she is today, whizzing past me with her friends at the rink. I think it's much the same for our DEI work. There are road hazards and occasionally the self-inflicted error or overcorrection that lands us on the pavement. But if we expect this, understand it as part of our development and journey, and know that people that care about us will help us up, we accrue confidence and experience.

I am a diversity researcher and educator and have held this role professionally for decades—but every day I learn new lessons about identity, power, and oppression. I am complicit at times in reifying structures that oppress or limit opportunity, but more often, I think I am doing the difficult work of dismantling those same structures. I know this is work I must engage in, with humility, in colleagueship with many others, and I suspect I will always be doing this. There's no clearer evidence of this than when I think of the range of learning environments I've been privileged to engage with—our "How to Talk with Your Kids About Race" workshop with parents of preschool and elementary aged children, to dialogues with the Osher Lifelong Learning Institutes (OLLI), whose minimum age is fifty.[10] In all of these environments I'm positioned as the instructor or facilitator, but I am eager for the moments of dissonance, reflection, and learning. I'm not going to pretend that every learning opportunity works on my schedule or that some don't smart and sting a bit in the moment, but you don't get to revel in the joy of a smooth free skate without accruing a bruise or two in the process.

My humble admonition to you, friend, is to keep skating. When you need time to heal, pause and take it. Surround yourself with fellow skaters (hopefully some who have been doing it for a while and some newer to it than you) who are simultaneously supportive and able to help you improve your stride. Learn how to maneuver around the road hazards and anticipate them. But most importantly, get out and skate. Take advantage of the opportunities and different venues in which you can express your personality and unique interests, and find joy in the work that will make our institutions more welcoming, more inclusive, and more hospitable. Share your journey, whether it's via traditional or social media, or just among friends. Reimagining an equitable and socially just world is courageous work, and somebody will be inspired by your reflections.

Restore and resist, and hopefully you will experience those fleeting moments of freedom and satisfaction . . . frequently.

Notes

FOREWORD

1. Melanie Wilcox, "Texas Legislators Introduce Bill Banning Diversity, Equity and Inclusion Programs at Public Universities," *Daily Caller*, December 16, 2022, https://dailycaller.com/2022/12/16/texas-legislators-introduce-bill-banning-diversity-equity-inclusion-programs-state-universities/.
2. Rev. James Cleveland, "I Feel No Ways Tired," on *King of Gospel* (Savoy Records, 1993), track 2, compact disc.
3. *Sense and Sensibility*, written by Andrew Davies (London: BBC, 2008).
4. bell hooks, *Teaching to Transgress: Education as the Practice of Freedom* (New York: Routledge, 1994), 34.
5. James Baldwin, *Giovanni's Room* (New York: Knopf Doubleday, 1956), 93.

INTRODUCTION

1. As quoted in Charles V. Willie and Richard J. Reddick, *A New Look at Black Families*, 6th ed. (Lanham, MD: Rowman & Littlefield, 2010), 3.
2. As cited in Laura Sherbin and Ripa Rashid, "Diversity Doesn't Stick Without Inclusion," *Harvard Business Review*, February 1, 2017, https://hbr.org/2017/02/diversity-doesnt-stick-without-inclusion.
3. Terrell Strayhorn, *College Students' Sense of Belonging: A Key to Educational Success for All* (New York: Routledge, 2012), 17.
4. Laura I. Rendón, "Validating Culturally Diverse Students: Toward a New Model of Learning and Student Development," *Innovative Higher Education* 19 (1994): 33–51.
5. Ahmed, *On Being Included*.
6. Uju Anya, Royel M. Johnson, and Liliana M. Garces, *Racial Equity on College Campuses: Connecting Research and Practice* (Albany: SUNY Press, 2022).
7. Beverly Daniel Tatum, *Why Are All the Black Kids Sitting Together in the Cafeteria?*, rev. ed. (New York: Basic Books, 2003), 4.
8. *BlacKkKlansman*, directed by Spike Lee (Focus Features, 2018), on Apple TV+, https://tv.apple.com/us/movie/blackkklansman/umc.cmc.537dty6z3xaadlo3yj6m22txm?action=play.

9. Joe R. Feagin and Hernán Vera, *White Racism: The Basics* (New York: Routledge, 2001), 17.
10. Joe R. Feagin, *Racist America: Roots, Current Realities, and Future Reparations* (New York: Routledge, 2001), 6.
11. Eduardo Bonilla-Silva, *White Supremacy and Racism in the Post-Civil Rights Era* (Boulder, CO: Lynne Rienner Publishers, 2001).
12. Robert Jensen, *The Heart of Whiteness: Confronting Race, Racism, and White Privilege* (San Francisco: City Lights Books, 2005), 3–4.
13. Wilder, *Ebony and Ivy*.
14. Jensen, *Heart of Whiteness*, 4.
15. Eduardo Bonilla-Silva, *Racism Without Racists: Color-Blind Racism and the Persistence of Racial Inequality in the United States* (Lanham, MD: Rowman & Littlefield, 2006).
16. Tatum, *Black Kids Sitting Together*.
17. Eula Biss, "White Debt," *New York Times Magazine*, December 6, 2015, https://www.nytimes.com/2015/12/06/magazine/white-debt.html.
18. Gloria Ladson-Billings, "From the Achievement Gap to the Education Debt: Understanding Achievement in U.S. Schools," *Educational Researcher* 35 no. 7 (October 2006): 3–12, https://www.jstor.org/stable/3876731.
19. The Boyer 2030 Commission, *The Equity/Excellence Imperative: A 2030 Blueprint for Undergraduate Education at U.S. Research Universities* (Fort Collins, CO: The Association for Undergraduate Education at Research Universities, 2022), 51, https://wac.colostate.edu/docs/books/boyer2030/report.pdf.
20. Mamta Accapadi, "From Reflection to Refraction," *New Directions for Student Services* 160 (Winter 2017): 101, https://onlinelibrary.wiley.com/doi/pdf/10.1002/ss.20246.

CHAPTER 1

1. Gladwell, *Outliers*, 221.
2. Nash, *Liberating Scholarly Writing*, 2.
3. Kindersley, "Muhammad Ali," 71.
4. *Journal of Restorative Resistance*; Phrie World, "Restorative Resistance."
5. Swaby, "Seeing You Through Her and Me," 38.
6. King, Jr., "Beyond Vietnam."
7. Musil, *Brats*.
8. PCS: permanent change of station. CONUS: continental United States. TDY: temporary duty.
9. Datla, *Leading with Empathy*.
10. Badger, "Study: Austin Segregated."
11. Cuban, *School Reform*.
12. Spence et al., "Structuring Race," 33–62.
13. McGee, "Students Forged a Friendship."
14. Lum, "Racial Sensitivity Programs," B1.

15. Karlamangla, "1992 Los Angeles Riots."
16. Shuford, "Flesh Tones and Feelings," 6–11.
17. Berkowitz, Jaschik, Ekland-Olson, and Reddick, interview by Conan.
18. Reddick, "Eliminating Inequalities."
19. Reddick, "Sankofa," 150–166.
20. Smith, "Plan to Rename School," B1.
21. Joseph, *The Third Reconstruction.*
22. Levin and Maisel, "'The Eyes of Texas' Controversy."
23. Eyes of Texas History Committee, "Committee Report."
24. Smith et al., "Interrupting the Usual," 133–160.
25. Canizales, "Impostor Syndrome."
26. Griffin and Reddick, "Surveillance and Sacrifice," 1032–1057.

CHAPTER 2

1. Kram, *Mentoring at Work.*
2. Thomas, "Race Matters," 98–107.
3. Levinson, *Seasons of a Man's Life.*
4. Margolis and Romero, "Functioning of the Hidden Curriculum," 1–33.
5. Beykont and Daiute, "Inclusiveness in Higher Education Courses," 35–42.
6. The University of Texas at Austin, "Provost's Distinguished Service Academy."
7. Griffin and Reddick, "Surveillance and Sacrifice," 1032–1057.
8. Johnson, *On Being a Mentor.*
9. Reddick, "Of Feral Faculty," 43–51.
10. Rockquemore, "A New Model of Mentoring."
11. Johnson, *On Being a Mentor.*
12. National Center for Education Statistics, "Race/Ethnicity of College Faculty."
13. National Center for Education Statistics, *The Condition of Education 2020.*
14. Padilla, "Ethnic Minority Scholars," 24–27.
15. Thomas, "Race Matters," 98–107.
16. Reddick and Pritchett, "Mentoring Relationships with Black Students," 54–84.
17. Reddick and Pritchett, 54–84.
18. Crisp, "College Student Mentoring Scale," 177–194.
19. Homans, "Social Behavior as Exchange," 597–606.
20. Society of Women Engineers, "Celebrating National Mentoring Month."
21. Reddick, "Navigating Developmental Relationships."
22. Reddick and Struve, "Mentorability."
23. Reddick, Griffin, and Cherwitz, "Answering Call for Mentoring," 54.
24. Reddick and Struve, "Mentorability," 3.
25. Gasman, "Faculty of Color."
26. Blake-Beard, Murrell, and Thomas, "Unfinished Business."
27. Black and Taylor, "Nobody's Talking to the Mentees," 606–626.
28. Black, "No One Is Talking to the Mentees."

29. Black.
30. *Seinfeld*, "The Fatigues."
31. Bennhold, "Another Side of #MeToo."
32. Kanter, *Men and Women*.
33. Khazan, "Dudely Dinners."
34. Reddick, "Mentoring in the #MeToo Era."
35. Reddick, "Mentoring in the #MeToo Era."
36. Reddick, "Stop Focusing on Their Hair."

CHAPTER 3

1. Joseph and Hirshfield, "Race and Cultural Taxation," 121–141.
2. Reddick, Bukoski, and Smith, "(Cultural) Taxation," 31–62.
3. Banks, "Scholars: Roles and Conflicts," 325–338.
4. Holmes IV, "When Scholarship Isn't Enough!" 668–675.
5. Miller et al., "Self-Care for Diversity Educators," 14–26.
6. Burns, "Recognize and Rescind Cultural Taxation."
7. Anderson, "Colleges as Courageous Spaces."
8. Foster, *Blackademics*.
9. Spivak, *Critique of Postcolonial Reason*.
10. Ali, "Black History Month."
11. Padilla, "Ethnic Minority Scholars," 24–27.
12. Padilla, 26.
13. Davis and Harper, "Beyoncé's 'Renaissance.'"
14. Gay, "Navigating Marginality," 265–288.
15. Stanley, "Coloring the Academic Landscape," 701–736.
16. Stanley, 701.
17. Joseph and Hirshfield, "Race and Cultural Taxation."
18. Reddick, Bukoski, and Smith, "(Cultural) Taxation," 47.
19. hooks, "Homeplace," 33–38.
20. Foster, *Blackademics*.
21. Gewin, "Time Tax."
22. Skop, Twitter.
23. Suarez, Twitter.
24. Sabbagh, Twitter.
25. Prescod-Weinstein, Twitter.
26. O'Meara et al., "Undoing Disparities," e0207316.
27. Meyerson, "Radical Change."
28. Willie, *Effective Education*.
29. Reddick, Bukoski, and Smith, "(Cultural) Taxation," 44.
30. Reddick and Sáenz, "Coming Home," 353–380.
31. Patton, "Home for the Holidays."
32. Reddick, "Reclaiming Our Time," 238–266.

33. Jenkins, "St Scholastica's Day Riot."
34. Taylor, "Urban Renewal, 'N–ro Removal.'"
35. Russell, "Unseen Power of the Ku Klux Klan," 1–35.
36. Reddick, "How Else Do You Eliminate Inequality?"
37. Reddick, Bukoski, and Smith, "(Cultural) Taxation," 42–43.
38. Reddick, Bukoski, and Smith, 42–43.
39. Despres, "Racism a Public Health Crisis!"
40. Reddick, "John Henryism."
41. Harris, "The Death of an Adjunct."
42. Catterall, Mickenberg, and Reddick, "Design Thinking," 34–47.
43. Catterall, Mickenberg, and Reddick.
44. Younger and Kalipeni, "Caregiving Crisis."
45. Lloyd, "One in Four Black Workers."
46. Thompson and Reddick, "Joe Harper Jr."
47. Reddick, Bukoski, and Smith, "(Cultural) Taxation."

CHAPTER 4

1. Reddick, "'Privilege Payoff.'"
2. Padilla, "Ethnic Minority Scholars," 24–27.
3. McIntosh, "White Privilege," 1–3.
4. Bob Jensen, personal conversation with author, 2014.
5. DeVega, "White Americans Support Welfare Programs."
6. DeVega.
7. Jan, "Biggest Beneficiaries."
8. Mettler, *The Submerged State.*
9. Baker et al., "Supporting Mid-Career Faculty."
10. Reddick, "'Privilege Payoff.'"
11. Guarino and Borden, "Service Loads and Gender," 672–694.
12. Reddick, "Shelters Through the Storm."
13. Karau and Williams, "Social Loafing," 681–706.
14. O'Meara et al., "Undoing Disparities," e0207316.
15. O'Meara et al., e0207316.
16. Reddick and Pritchett, "Mentoring Relationships with Black Students," 54–84.
17. Reddick, "Shelters Through the Storm."
18. Reddick.
19. Davis, *De Colores*, x.
20. Matthew, *Written/Unwritten.*
21. Tervalon and Murray-Garcia, "Cultural Humility," 117–125.
22. Tervalon and Murray-Garcia, 117–125.
23. Tervalon and Murray-Garcia.
24. Yosso, "Whose Culture Has Capital?" 69–91.
25. Spivak, *Critique of Postcolonial Reason.*

26. Williams, Berger, and McClendon, *Inclusive Excellence and Change.*
27. King, Jr., "Quest for Peace and Justice."
28. Zamudio-Suarez, "Race on Campus."
29. Zamudio-Suarez.
30. Bunsis and Witt, "Administrative Costs."
31. State Higher Education Finance, "State Funding"; Featherman, "Why College Costs So Much."
32. Friedersdorf, "Diversity Bureaucracy."
33. Bell, Twitter.
34. Gitlin, "Water Buffalo Incident."
35. Hingston, "Political Correctness."
36. Matthews, *Bright College Years.*
37. Airaksinen, "'Diversity Educators.'"
38. Cuarón, *Prisoner of Azkaban.*

CHAPTER 5

1. *The Jargon File.*
2. Bolman and Deal, *Reframing Organizations.*
3. Brown-Nagin, *Legacy of Slavery.*
4. Wilder, *Ebony and Ivy.*
5. President's Commission on Slavery and the University, "Universities Studying Slavery."
6. Rittel and Webber, "Dilemmas."
7. Rittel and Webber, 156.
8. Rittel and Webber, 160.
9. Rittel and Webber.
10. Malloy and Schwartz, "Biden Widens Lead."
11. Watkins, "UT-Austin Removes Confederate Statues"; Wendland, "Lee Statue's Removal"; Small, "Richmond's Confederate Statues."
12. Reddick et al., "Taxation and Representation."
13. Reddick and Sáenz, "Coming Home," 353–380.
14. Reddick and Sáenz, 363.
15. Wells, "School Song's Past."
16. Berry, *Traditions and Nostalgia.*
17. Southern, *Music of Black Americans.*
18. Justin, "Football Players."
19. Williford, "Student Petitions."
20. McCann, "UT Frats."
21. "DDCE's Biggest Milestones."
22. Martin, "Future of Confederate Statue."
23. Knich, "Simkins' Name Removed."
24. Najmabadi and Andu, "Greg Fenves Leaving."

25. Hartzell, "Listening Closely."
26. Hartzell, "Diverse and Welcoming Campus."
27. Office of the President, "The Eyes of Texas History Committee."
28. Wood, "New Leader"; Lavergne, *Before* Brown.
29. Deutser, "Meet Brad."
30. Davis, "Sam Ehlinger Explains."
31. McGee, "'UT Needs Rich Donors.'"
32. According to Norma H. Wolff, "A dashiki is a loose fitting, pullover shirt usually sewn from colorful, African-inspired cotton prints . . . appear[ing] during the 1960s when embraced by the black pride and white counterculture movements." I own many and frequently wear them at work. "Dashiki," Love to Know, https://fashion-history.lovetoknow.com/clothing-types-styles/dashiki.
33. Kipling, "If."
34. Reddick and Vincent, "Black Youth."
35. Eyes of Texas History Committee, "Committee Report."
36. Eyes of Texas History Committee.
37. Eyes of Texas History Committee, 18.
38. Eyes of Texas History Committee, 2.
39. Meyerson, "Radical Change."
40. Jayakumar and Museus, "Campus Cultures," 2.
41. Jayakumar and Museus, 14–17.
42. Jayakumar and Museus, 19.

CHAPTER 6

1. Ecarma, "FBI Director."
2. Erenrich, *Cost of Freedom*; Giles, "Race, Social Justice."
3. Zamudio-Suarez, "Race on Campus."
4. Dobbin and Kalev, "Diversity Training," 48–55.
5. Miller et al., "Self-Care for Diversity Educators," 14–26.
6. United Nations, "Sustainability."
7. Fitness Institute of Texas, "Get FIT."
8. Kaur, "Jumping for Joy."
9. Fisher, "Cultural Humility," 53–66.
10. Huston-Tillotson University, "Symposium on Race Unity."
11. Burns, "Conversation with Reddick."
12. Kay Pranis, *Guide for Implementing the Balanced and Restorative Justice Model*, Office of Juvenile Justice and Delinquency Prevention (Washington, DC: US Department of Justice, 1998), https://www.ojp.gov/pdffiles/167887.pdf.
13. Nieto, "Placing Equity,"185.
14. Ali, *Safe Spaces*, 8.
15. Ahmed, *On Being Included*, 3.
16. Bollinger, "Diversity in Higher Education," 431–436.

17. Flier, "Against Diversity Statements."
18. Canning and Reddick, "Defense of Diversity Statements."
19. Canning and Reddick.
20. Meyerson, "Radical Change," 7.
21. Kezar, Gallant, and Lester, "Everyday People," 129–151.
22. Meyerson, *Tempered Radicals.*
23. Meyerson.
24. Reddick, Bukoski, and Smith, "Tempered Radicalism," 176–192.
25. Canizales, "Impostor Syndrome."
26. Fallows, "Worst Year"; Hooks, "Significance of the BLM Protests."
27. Kurlansky, *1968.*
28. McClure, "Don't Blame the Pandemic."
29. James, "John Henryism," 163–182.
30. Obama, *Becoming.*
31. Reddick, "John Henryism."
32. University Innovation Alliance, "Cultural Taxation."
33. Reddick et al., "Academic Fathers," 1–15.
34. Albert O. Hirschman, *Exit, Voice, and Loyalty: Responses to Decline in Firms, Organizations, and States* (Cambridge, MA: Harvard University Press, 1970).
35. McDonald, "Greatest of All Time."
36. Team USA, Twitter.
37. Carayol, "Simone Biles."
38. Barrett, "Simone Biles to Congress"; Cacciola and Mather, "Larry Nassar Sentencing."
39. Goertzen, "Kirk, Morgan Slam Biles."
40. Chozick and Parker, "Trump's Gender-Based Attacks."
41. Attiah, "Men Need to Learn."
42. Bailey, *Misogynoir Transformed.*
43. Clarey and Rothenberg, "Osaka Withdraws from Wimbledon."
44. Reddick, "Reclaiming Our Time," 258.
45. William Ernest Henley, "Invictus." Poetry Foundation, 2022, https://www.poetryfoundation.org/poems/51642/invictus.

CONCLUSION

1. Marybeth Gasman and Ufuoma Abiola, "Black and White: Making Cross-Race Mentoring Work and Work Well," *Diverse Issues in Higher Education*, April 24, 2012, https://www.diverseeducation.com/opinion/article/15092037/black-and-white-making-cross-race-mentoring-work-and-work-well.
2. Ellie Silverman and Teo Armus, "5 Years After Deadly Rally, Charlottesville Wants to Tell Its Own Story," *Washington Post*, August 12, 2022, https://www.washingtonpost.com/dc-md-va/2022/08/12/charlottesville-unite-right-five-years/.

3. UTRGV News and Internal Communications, "Dr. Juliet V. Garcia to Receive The Presidential Medal of Freedom," *The Newsroom*, July 1, 2022, https://www.utrgv.edu/newsroom/2022/07/01-dr-juliet-v-garcia-to-receive-the-presidential-medal-of-freedom.htm.
4. "Taking Responsibility for Systemic Racism," interview with Charles "Chip" Gallagher, Lisa Bond, and Andrew Sullivan, interview by Jon Stewart, *The Problem with Jon Stewart*, Apple TV+, https://www.youtube.com/watch?v=1cmnwbGmu7w.
5. "Taking Responsibility," interview.
6. Richard V. Reeves, *Dream Hoarders: How the American Upper Middle Class Is Leaving Everyone Else in the Dust, Why That Is a Problem, And What to Do About It* (Washington, DC: Brookings Institution Press, 2018).
7. Mariana Avetisyan and Shushanna Grigoryan, "Psychological Characteristics of Consumer Behavior," *Main Issues of Pedagogy and Psychology* 21, no. 1 (2022): 6–11, https://doi.org/10.24234/miopap.v21i1.421.
8. Z Nicolazzo, "Imagining a Trans* Epistemology: What Liberation Thinks Like in Postsecondary Education," *Urban Education* 56, no. 3 (2021): 511–536.
9. James Baldwin and William F. Buckley, "Has the American Dream Been Achieved at the Expense of the Negro?" The Cambridge Union, filmed by NET, February 18, 1965, video of debate, 58:35, https://www.youtube.com/watch?v=5Tek9h3a5wQ.
10. Lamiyah Bahrainwala, Roberto German, Katie Malinski, and Richard J. Reddick, "How to Talk to Your Kids About Race," Panel Presentation for Russell Lee Elementary School Parent-Teacher Association, December 18, 2018; "About UT OLLI," Osher Lifelong Learning Institute–The University of Texas at Austin, 2022, https://olli.utexas.edu/about.

Bibliography

Ahmed, Sara. On *Being Included: Racism and Diversity in Institutional Life*. Durham, NC: Duke University Press, 2012.

Airaksinen, Toni. "'Diversity Educators' Fear 'Burnout' from 'Microaggressions.'" *Campus Reform*, October 6, 2017. https://www.campusreform.org/article?id=9924.

Albert O. Hirschman. Exit, *Voice, and Loyalty: Responses to Decline in Firms, Organizations, and States*. Cambridge, MA: Harvard University Press, 1970.

Ali, Diana. *Safe Spaces and Brave Spaces: Historical Context and Recommendations for Student Affairs Professionals*. Washington, DC: NASPA Research and Policy Institute, 2017. https://www.naspa.org/images/uploads/main/Policy_and_Practice_No_2_Safe_Brave_Spaces.pdf.

Ali, Rasha. "Here's How NOT to Celebrate Black History Month, and What You Can Do Instead." *USA Today*, February 19, 2019. https://eu.usatoday.com/story/life/2019/02/19/black-history-month-food-how-you-should-and-shouldnt-celebrate/2869881002/.

Anderson, Jill. "Colleges as Courageous Spaces." *Harvard EdCast*, October 30, 2019. https://www.gse.harvard.edu/news/19/10/harvard-edcast-colleges-courageous-spaces.

Attiah, Karen. "What Men Need to Learn from Simone Biles." *Washington Post*, July 29, 2021. https://www.washingtonpost.com/opinions/2021/07/29/biles-is-helping-show-way-mental-health-lets-hope-follow-male-athletes-follow-her-lead/.

Badger, Emily. "Study: Austin Is Most Economically Segregated Metro Area." *Texas Tribune*, February 23, 2015. https://www.texastribune.org/2015/02/23/austin-most-economically-segregated-metro-area/.

Bailey, Moya. *Misogynoir Transformed: Black Women's Digital Resistance*. New York: NYU Press, 2021.

Baker, Vicki, Jaime Lester, Richard J. Reddick, and Aimee LaPointe Terosky. "Supporting Mid-Career Faculty: A Hands-On Session for Assuming Agency" (presentation). Association for the Study of Higher Education (ASHE) Council for the Advancement of Higher Education Programs (CAHEP), Tampa, FL, November 15, 2018.

Banks, William M. "Afro-American Scholars in the University: Roles and Conflicts." *American Behavioral Scientist* 27, no. 3 (1984): 325–338.

Barrett, Devlin. "Simone Biles to Congress: 'I Blame Larry Nassar, and I Also Blame an Entire System.'" *Washington Post*, September 15, 2021. https://www.washingtonpost.com/national-security/gymnasts-nassar-fbi-investigation-hearing/2021/09/14/de4832cc-159f-11ec-9589-31ac3173c2e5_story.html.

Bell, Monica (@*monicacbell*). Twitter, October 20, 2021, 1:50 p.m. https://twitter.com/monicacbell/status/1450897114960171018.

Bennhold, Katrin. "Another Side of #MeToo: Male Managers Fearful of Mentoring Women." *New York Times*, January 27, 2019. https://www.nytimes.com/2019/01/27/world/europe/metoo-backlash-gender-equality-davos-men.html.

Berkowitz, Jeremy, Scott Jaschik, Sheldon Ekland-Olson, and Rich Reddick. "Diversity on Campus." Interview by Neal Conan. *Talk of the Nation*, NPR, June 23, 2004. http://www.npr.org/templates/story/story.php?storyId=1972037.

Berry, Margaret C. *UT Austin Traditions and Nostalgia*. Fort Worth, TX: Eakins Press, 1992.

Beykont, Zeynep, and Colette Daiute. "Inclusiveness in Higher Education Courses: International Student Perspectives." *Equity & Excellence in Education* 35, no. 1 (2002): 35–42.

Black, Victoria G. "No One Is Talking to the Mentees." Filmed November 2018 in San Marcos, TX. TEDxTexasStateUniversity video, 11:35. https://www.ted.com/talks/victoria_black_no_one_is_talking_to_the_mentees.

Black, Victoria G., and Zachary W. Taylor. "Nobody's Talking to the Mentees." *Mentoring and Tutoring* 26, no. 5 (2018): 606–626.

Blake-Beard, Stacy, Audrey J. Murrell, and David A. Thomas. "Unfinished Business: The Impact of Race on Understanding Mentoring Relationships." Working paper, *Organizational Behavior*, July 2016. https://citeseerx.ist.psu.edu/viewdoc/download?doi=10.1.1.734.4904&rep=rep1&type=pdf.

Bollinger, Lee C. "The Need for Diversity in Higher Education." *Academic Medicine* 78, no. 5 (2003): 431–436.

Bolman, Lee, and Terry Deal. *Reframing Organizations: Artistry, Choice, and Leadership*. San Francisco, CA: Jossey-Bass, 2008.

Brown-Nagin, Tomiko. (chair). *Report of the Presidential Committee on Harvard and the Legacy of Slavery*. Cambridge, MA: Harvard Radcliffe Institute, April 25, 2022. https://legacyofslavery.harvard.edu/report/.

Bunsis, Howard, and David Witt. "Administrative Costs Rise as State Support Dwindles." AAUP Updates. August 27, 2010. https://www.aaup.org/news/administrative-costs-rise-state-support-dwindles.

Burns, Bridget K. "How to Recognize and Rescind Cultural Taxation: A Conversation with Richard Reddick, Professor and Associate Dean, University of Texas at Austin." *The UIA Blog*, April 29, 2021. https://theuia.org/blog/post/scholarship-2-practice-10-22-20-episode-richard-reddick-university-of-texas-austin.

———. "Interview with Dr. Richard Reddick from the University of Texas at Austin." In *The Innovating Together Podcast*, February 1, 2021. Audio, 33:19. https://podcasts.apple.com/us/podcast/interview-with-dr-richard-reddick-from-the/id1519140735?i=1000507326872.

Cacciola, Scott, and Victor Mather. "Larry Nassar Sentencing: 'I Just Signed Your Death Warrant.'" *New York Times*, January 24, 2018. https://www.nytimes.com/2018/01/24/sports/larry-nassar-sentencing.html.

Canizales, Anna. "UT Professor Says Impostor Syndrome Burdens Students on Campus, Affects Mental Health." *Daily Texan*, February 4, 2020. https://thedailytexan.com/2020/02/04/ut-professor-says-impostor-syndrome-burdens-students-on-campus-affects-mental-health/.

Canning, Charlotte M., and Richard J. Reddick. "In Defense of Diversity Statements." *Chronicle of Higher Education Review*, January 11, 2019. https://www.chronicle.com/article/in-defense-of-diversity-statements/.

Carayol, Tumaini. "Simone Biles to Take 'A Day at a Time' Before Further Tokyo Participation." *Guardian*, July 27, 2021. https://www.theguardian.com/sport/2021/jul/27/simon-biles-take-day-at-a-time-before-further-tokyo-olympics-participation.

Catterall, Kate M., Julia L. Mickenberg, and Richard J. Reddick. "Design Thinking, Collaborative Innovation, and Neoliberal Disappointment: Cruel Optimism in the History and Future of Higher Education." *Radical Teacher: A Socialist, Feminist, and Anti-Racist Journal on the Theory and Practice of Teaching* 114 (2019): 34–47.

Chozick, Amy, and Ashley Parker. "Donald Trump's Gender-Based Attacks on Hillary Clinton Have Calculated Risk." *New York Times*, April 28, 2016. https://www.nytimes.com/2016/04/29/us/politics/hillary-clinton-donald-trump-women.html.

Clarey, Christopher, and Ben Rothenberg. "Naomi Osaka Withdraws from Wimbledon but Will Play in Tokyo Olympics." *New York Times*, June 17, 2021. https://www.nytimes.com/2021/06/17/sports/tennis/naomi-osaka-withdraws-wimbledon-olympics.html.

Crisp, Gloria. "Conceptualization and Initial Validation of the College Student Mentoring Scale (CSMS)." *Journal of College Student Development* 50, no. 2 (2009): 177–194.

Cuarón, Alfonso, dir. *Harry Potter and the Prisoner of Azkaban*. Burbank, CA: Warner Bros. Pictures, 2004. DVD.

Cuban, Larry. *As Good as It Gets: What School Reform Brought to Austin*. Cambridge, MA: Harvard University Press, 2010.

Datla, Anjani. *Leading with Empathy: Tarana Burke and the Making of the Me Too Movement*. Cambridge, MA: Harvard Kennedy School of Government, 2006.

Davis, Angela Y. Foreword to *De Colores Means All of Us: Latina Views for a Multi-Colored Century* by Elizabeth Martinez, x. New York: Verso Books, 1988.

Davis, Danny. "After a 'Misunderstanding' in Dallas, Sam Ehlinger Explains Why He Stayed for 'The Eyes of Texas'." HookEm.com. October 20, 2020. https://www

.hookem.com/2020/10/20/misunderstanding-dallas-sam-ehlinger-explains-stayed-eyes-texas/.

Davis, Lori Patton, and Shaun Harper. "Beyoncé's 'Renaissance' is Music to These Black Scholars' Ears." Interview by Celeste Headlee. *Here & Now*, NPR, July 29, 2022. https://www.wbur.org/hereandnow/2022/07/29/beyonce-renaissance.

"DDCE's Biggest Milestones." *Access & Excellence*, 2017. https://web.archive.org/web/20170922004432/https://diversity.utexas.edu/wp-content/uploads/AccessIssue4Web.pdf.

Despres, Cliff. "Update: 246 Cities, Counties, Leaders Declare Racism a Public Health Crisis!" Salud America! September 1, 2021. https://salud-america.org/rising-number-of-cities-counties-are-declaring-racism-a-public-health-crisis/.

Deutser, Brad. "Meet Brad." About. 2022. https://www.braddeutser.com/about/.

DeVega, Chauncey. "White Americans Support Welfare Programs—but Only for Themselves, Says New Research." *Salon*, August 1, 2018. https://www.salon.com/2018/08/01/white-americans-support-welfare-programs-but-only-for-themselves-says-new-research/.

Dobbin, Frank, and Alexandra Kalev. "Why Doesn't Diversity Training Work? The Challenge for Industry and Academia." *Anthropology Now* 10, no. 2 (2018): 48–55.

Ecarma, Caleb. "The FBI Director Just Blew Up Team Trump's Anti-Antifa War Plan." *Vanity Fair*, September 17, 2020. https://www.vanityfair.com/news/2020/09/fbi-director-chris-wray-blew-up-trumps-anti-antifa-war-plan.

Erenrich, Susan J., ed. *The Cost of Freedom: Voicing a Movement After Kent State 1970*. Kent, OH: Kent State University Press, 2020.

Eyes of Texas History Committee. "The Eyes of Texas History Committee Report." March 9, 2021. https://eyesoftexas.utexas.edu/full-report/.

Fallows, James. "Is This the Worst Year in Modern American History? Comparing 2020 to 1968 Offers Some Disquieting Lessons for the Present." *Atlantic*, May 31, 2020. https://www.theatlantic.com/ideas/archive/2020/05/1968-and-2020-lessons-from-americas-worst-year-so-far/612415/.

Featherman, Sandra. "Why College Costs So Much." *New York Times* Archive, 2004. https://archive.nytimes.com/www.nytimes.com/ref/college/ll_pres_featherman.html.

Fisher, Emily S. "Cultural Humility as a Form of Social Justice: Promising Practices for Global School Psychology Training." *School Psychology International* 41, no. 1 (February 2020): 53–66.

Fitness Institute of Texas. "Get FIT." https://sites.edb.utexas.edu/fit/get-fit/.

Flier, Jeffrey. "Against Diversity Statements." *Chronicle of Higher Education Review*, January 3, 2019. https://www.chronicle.com/article/against-diversity-statements/.

Foster, Kevin, dir. *Blackademics*. Season 6, episode 5, "'Ultimately, It's About Love': How Black Faculty Navigate the White Academy." Aired June 17, 2018, on PBS. https://video.austinpbs.org/video/reddick-fox-foster-t8ulbm/.

Friedersdorf, Conor. "A Worrisome Peek Inside Yale Law's Diversity Bureaucracy." *Atlantic*, October 20, 2021. https://www.theatlantic.com/ideas/archive/2021/10/yale-law-diversity-bureaucrats-made-five-mistakes/620428/.

Gasman, Marybeth. "An Ivy League Professor on Why Colleges Don't Hire More Faculty of Color: 'We Don't Want Them.'" *Washington Post*, September 26, 2016. https://www.washingtonpost.com/news/grade-point/wp/2016/09/26/an-ivy-league-professor-on-why-colleges-dont-hire-more-faculty-of-color-we-dont-want-them/.

Gay, Geneva. "Navigating Marginality en Route to the Professoriate: Graduate Students of Color Learning and Living in Academia." *International Journal of Qualitative Studies in Education* 17, no. 2 (2004): 265–288.

Gewin, Virginia. "The Time Tax Put on Scientists of Colour: The Pressure on Researchers from Ethnic Minority Groups to Participate in Campus Diversity Issues Comes at a Cost." *Nature*, June 24, 2020. https://www.nature.com/articles/d41586-020-01920-6.

Giles, Mark S. "Race, Social Justice, and the Jackson State University Shootings." In *Historically Black Colleges and Universities*, edited by Marybeth Gasman and Christopher L. Tudico, 105–120. New York: Palgrave Macmillan, 2008.

Gitlin, Lara. "The Water Buffalo Incident through Eyes of Jacobowitz." *Daily Pennsylvanian*, April 15, 2003. https://www.thedp.com/article/2003/04/the_water_buffalo_incident_through_eyes_of_jacobowitz.

Gladwell, Malcolm. *Outliers: The Story of Success*. New York: Penguin, 2008.

Goertzen, Brenley. "Charlie Kirk, Piers Morgan Slam Simone Biles as a 'Selfish Sociopath' and 'Shame to the Country'." *Salon*, July 28, 2021. https://www.salon.com/2021/07/28/charlie-kirk-piers-morgan-slam-simone-biles-shes-a-selfish-sociopath-shame-to-the-country/.

Griffin, Kimberly A., and Richard J. Reddick. "Surveillance and Sacrifice: Gender Differences in the Mentoring Patterns of Black Professors at Predominantly White Research Universities." *American Educational Research Journal* 48, no. 5 (2011): 1032–1057.

Guarino, Cassandra M., and Victor M. H. Borden. "Faculty Service Loads and Gender: Are Women Taking Care of the Academic Family?" *Research in Higher Education* 58, no. 6 (2017): 672–694.

Harris, Adam. "The Death of an Adjunct." *Atlantic*, April 8, 2019. https://www.theatlantic.com/education/archive/2019/04/adjunct-professors-higher-education-thea-hunter/586168/.

Hartzell, Jay. "Listening Closely and Moving Forward Together." June 15, 2020. https://president.utexas.edu/messages-speeches-2020/listening-closely-and-moving-forward-together.

———. "A More Diverse and Welcoming Campus," July 13, 2020. https://president.utexas.edu/messages-speeches-2020/a-more-diverse-and-welcoming-campus.

Hingston, Sandy. "A History of Political Correctness: 20 Years After Penn's 'Water Buffalo' Incident." *Philadelphia Magazine*, April 26, 2013. https://www.phillymag.com/news/2013/04/26/penns-water-buffalo-incident-20-years/.

Holmes IV, Oscar. "For Diversity Scholars Who Have Considered Activism When Scholarship Isn't Enough!" *Equality, Diversity and Inclusion: An International Journal* 38, no. 6 (2019): 668–675.

Homans, George C. "Social Behavior as Exchange." *American Journal of Sociology* 63, no. 6 (1958): 597–606.

hooks, bell. "Homeplace: A Site of Resistance." In *Undoing Place? A Geographical Reader*, edited by Linda McDowell, 33–38. London: Routledge, 2020.

Hooks, Christopher. "Black Studies Scholar Peniel Joseph on the Significance of the BLM Protests: How Educational Developers Can Broker Discourse on Black Faculty Lives in the #BlackLivesMatter Era." *To Improve the Academy: A Journal of Educational Development* 39, no. 1 (2020): 31–62.

———. "The UT Professor Sees Echoes of the Past—and Hope for the Future—in the Demonstrations Rocking the Nation." *Texas Monthly*, June 10, 2020. https://www.texasmonthly.com/news-politics/peniel-joseph-black-lives-matter-protests/.

Huston-Tillotson University. "2022 Louis Gregory Symposium on Race Unity." Academic Calendar. April 22, 2022. https://htu.edu/47900/2022-louis-gregory-symposium-on-race-unity.

James, Sherman A. "John Henryism and the Health of African-Americans." *Culture, Medicine and Psychiatry* 18 (1994): 163–182.

Jan, Tracy. "The Biggest Beneficiaries of the Government Safety Net: Working-Class Whites." *Washington Post*, February 16, 2017. https://www.washingtonpost.com/news/wonk/wp/2017/02/16/the-biggest-beneficiaries-of-the-government-safety-net-working-class-whites/.

The Jargon File (version 4.2.2.) August 20, 2000. https://vanderworp.org/wp-content/uploads/2019/06/jargon.pdf.

Jaschik, Scott. "The Professor Who Wasn't Fired." *Inside Higher Education*, July 1, 2015. https://www.insidehighered.com/news/2015/07/01/twitter-explodes-false-reports-u-memphis-fired-professor-why.

Jayakumar, Uma, and Sam Museus. "Mapping the Intersection of Campus Cultures and Equitable Outcomes Among Racially Diverse Student Populations." In *Creating Campus Cultures: Fostering Success Among Racially Diverse Student Populations*, edited by Uma Jayakumar and Sam Museus, 1–27. New York: Routledge, 2012.

Jenkins, Stephanie. "St Scholastica's Day Riot, Oxford, 1355: The Riot, and Its Consequences for the Next Five Hundred Years." Oxford History: Mayors & Lord Mayors. http://www.oxfordhistory.org.uk/mayors/government/scholastica.html.

Johnson, W. Brad. *On Being a Mentor: A Guide for Higher Education Faculty*. New York: Routledge, 2015.

Joseph, Peniel E. *The Third Reconstruction: America's Struggle for Racial Justice in the Twenty-First Century*. New York: Basic Books, 2022.

Joseph, Tiffany D., and Laura E. Hirshfield. "'Why Don't You Get Somebody New to Do It?' Race and Cultural Taxation in the Academy." *Ethnic and Racial Studies* 34, no. 1 (2011): 121–141.

Journal of Restorative Resistance. "Join the Journal of Restorative Resistance for the launch of its very first issue! #AdvocacythroughResearch #RestorativeResistance." December 19, 2019, 10:30 AM. https://web.archive.org/web/20230309222652/https://twitter.com/TheJournalofRR/status/1201176858915737600?cxt=HHwWgMC8wab_t6shAAAA.

Justin, Raga. "UT-Austin Football Players Demand School Rename Buildings Named After Racist Figures, Donate to Black Lives Matter." *Texas Tribune*, June 12, 2020. https://www.texastribune.org/2020/06/12/ut-austin-football-players-buildings-racism/.

Kanter, Rosabeth Moss. *Men and Women of the Corporation*. New York: Basic Books, 2008.

Karau, Steven J., and Kipling D. Williams. "Social Loafing: A Meta-Analytic Review and Theoretical Integration." *Journal of Personality and Social Psychology* 65, no. 4 (1993): 681–706.

Karlamangla, Soumya. "Remembering the 1992 Los Angeles Riots: A Reporter Who Covered the Riots Reflects 30 Years Later." *New York Times*, May 6, 2022. https://www.nytimes.com/2022/05/06/us/los-angeles-riots.html.

Kaur, Minreet. "I Used to Hate Exercise, but with Support from My Parents, I'm Now Jumping for Joy." *Guardian*, November 21, 2021. https://www.theguardian.com/lifeandstyle/2021/nov/14/i-used-to-hate-exercise-but-with-support-from-my-parents-i-am-now-jumping-for-joy.

Kezar, Adriana, Tricia Bertram Gallant, and Jaime Lester. "Everyday People Making a Difference on College Campuses: The Tempered Grassroots Leadership Tactics of Faculty and Staff." *Studies in Higher Education* 36, no. 2 (2011): 129–151.

Khazan, Olga. "How Pence's Dudely Dinners Hurt Women." *Atlantic*, March 20, 2017. https://www.theatlantic.com/science/archive/2017/03/pences-gender-segregated-dinners/521286/.

Kindersley, Dorling. "Muhammad Ali." In *Timelines from Black History: Leaders, Legends, Legacies*, 71. New York: Penguin Random House, 2021.

King, Martin Luther, Jr. "Beyond Vietnam—A Time to Break Silence" (speech). New York, April 4, 1967. American Rhetoric. https://www.americanrhetoric.com/speeches/mlkatimetobreaksilence.htm.

———. "The Quest for Peace and Justice" (speech). Oslo, Norway, December 11, 1964. The Nobel Prize. https://www.nobelprize.org/prizes/peace/1964/king/lecture/.

Kipling, J. Rudyard. "If" (1943). Poetry Foundation. https://www.poetryfoundation.org/poems/46473/if—.

Knich, Diane. "Simkins' Name Removed from Dorm." *Post and Courier*, July 25, 2010. https://www.postandcourier.com/news/simkins-name-removed-from-dorm/article_4ecd40f3-c588-5166-88a6-e1eb8d21d716.html.

Kram, Kathy E. *Mentoring at Work: Developmental Relationships in Organizational Life*. Lanham, MD: University Press of America, 1988.

Kurlansky, Mark. *1968: The Year that Rocked the World*. London: Vintage Books, 2004.

Lavergne, Gary M. *Before* Brown*: Heman Marion Sweatt, Thurgood Marshall, and the Long Road to Justice*. Austin: University of Texas Press, 2010.

Levin, Joe, and Ivan Maisel. "Behind the Scenes of UT's 'The Eyes of Texas' Controversy." *Texas Monthly*, May 2021. https://www.texasmonthly.com/news-politics/behind-the-scenes-of-uts-the-eyes-of-texas-controversy/.

Levinson, Daniel J. *The Seasons of a Man's Life*. New York: Random House, 1978.

Lloyd, Camille. "One in Four Black Workers Report Discrimination at Work." *Gallup*, January 12, 2021. https://news.gallup.com/poll/328394/one-four-black-workers-report-discrimination-work.aspx.

Lum, Lydia. "Westlake High School Sponsoring Racial Sensitivity Programs." *Austin American-Statesman*, January 28, 1990. B1.

Malloy, Tim, and Doug Schwartz. *Biden Widens Lead over Trump to 15 Points in Presidential Race, Quinnipiac University National Poll Finds; Trump Job Approval Rating Drops to 36 Percent*. Hamden, CT: Quinnipiac University, July 15, 2020. https://poll.qu.edu/images/polling/us/us07152020_ulvz33.pdf.

Margolis, Eric, and Mary Romero. "'The Department is Very Male, Very White, Very Old, and Very Conservative': The Functioning of the Hidden Curriculum in Graduate Sociology Departments." *Harvard Educational Review* 68, no. 1 (1988): 1–33.

Martin, Brittney. "UT Austin President Forms a Committee to Discuss Future of Confederate Statue on Campus." *Dallas Morning News*, June 23, 2015. https://www.dallasnews.com/news/politics/2015/06/23/ut-austin-president-forms-a-committee-to-discuss-future-of-confederate-statue-on-campus/.

Matthew, Patricia A., ed. *Written/Unwritten: Diversity and the Hidden Truths of Tenure*. Chapel Hill: UNC Press Books, 2016.

Matthews, Anne. *Bright College Years: Inside the American Campus Today*. Chicago, IL: University of Chicago Press, 1997.

McCann, Mac. "Do UT Frats Have a Race Problem? Longtime Longhorn Sees Some Improvement; Room for More." *Austin Chronicle*, March 27, 2015. https://www.austinchronicle.com/news/2015-03-27/do-ut-frats-have-a-race-problem/.

McClure, Kevin R. "Don't Blame the Pandemic for Worker Discontent: It Hasn't Just Been a Tough Two Years. It's Been a Tough Two Decades." *Chronicle of Higher Education*, May 27, 2022. https://www.chronicle.com/article/dont-blame-the-pandemic-for-worker-discontent.

McDonald, Scott. "Simone Biles Called Herself the Greatest of All Time. Is She?" *Newsweek*, July 27, 2021. https://www.newsweek.com/simone-biles-called-herself-greatest-all-time-she-1613768.

McGee, Kate. "These Students Forged a Friendship in Austin's 'Golden Age' of Integration." KUT 90.5 Austin's NPR Station. May 16, 2014. https://www.kut.org/education/2014-05-16/these-students-forged-a-friendship-in-austins-golden-age-of-integration.

———. "'UT Needs Rich Donors': Emails Show Wealthy Alumni Supporting 'Eyes of Texas' Threatened to Pull Donations." *Texas Tribune*, March 1, 2021. https://www.texastribune.org/2021/03/01/ut-eyes-of-texas-donors-emails/.

McIntosh, Peggy. "White Privilege: Unpacking the Invisible Knapsack." *Peace and Freedom* (July/August 1989): 1–3.

Mettler, Suzanne. *The Submerged State: How Invisible Government Policies Undermine American Democracy*. Chicago, IL: University of Chicago Press, 2011.

Meyerson, Debra E. "Radical Change, The Quiet Way." *Harvard Business Review*, October 2001. https://hbr.org/2001/10/radical-change-the-quiet-way.

———. *Tempered Radicals: How People Use Difference to Inspire Change at Work*. Cambridge, MA: Harvard Business School Press, 2001.

Miller, Ryan A., Veronica A. Jones, Richard J. Reddick, Tracie Lowe, Brandelyn Franks Flunder, Kristen Hogan, and Ana Ixchel Rosal. "Educating Through Microaggressions: Self-Care for Diversity Educators." *Journal of Student Affairs Research and Practice* 55, no. 1 (2018): 14–26.

Musil, Donna, dir. *Brats: Our Journey Home*. Brats Without Borders, 2006. DVD.

Najmabadi, Shannon, and Naomi Andu. "With Greg Fenves Leaving, UT-Austin Loses 'Steady' Hand in Unsteady Times." *Texas Tribune*, April 7, 2020. https://www.texastribune.org/2020/04/07/pandemic-upends-higher-education-ut-austin-president-greg-fenves-exits/.

Nash, Robert J. *Liberating Scholarly Writing: The Power of Personal Narrative*. New York: Teachers College Press, 2004.

National Center for Education Statistics. *The Condition of Education 2020: College Enrollment Rates*. Washington, DC: US Department of Education, 2019. https://nces.ed.gov/programs/coe/pdf/coe_cpb.pdf.

———. "Fast Facts: Race/Ethnicity of College Faculty." Institute of Education Sciences. US Department of Education, 2020. https://nces.ed.gov/fastfacts/display.asp?id=61#:~

Nieto, Sonia. "Placing Equity Front and Center: Some Thoughts on Transforming Teacher Education for a New Century." *Journal of Teacher Education* 51, no. 3 (May/June 2000): 185.

Obama, Michelle. *Becoming*. New York: Crown Publishing, 2018.

Office of Juvenile Justice and Delinquency Prevention. *Guide for Implementing the Balanced and Restorative Justice Model*, principal writer Kay Pranis. Washington, DC: US Department of Justice, 1998. https://www.ojp.gov/pdffiles/167887.pdf.

Office of the President, "The Eyes of Texas History Committee." November 2020. https://president.utexas.edu/eyes-texas-history-committee.

O'Meara, KerryAnn, Audrey Jaeger, Joya Misra, Courtney Lennartz, and Alexandra Kuvaeva. "Undoing Disparities in Faculty Workloads: A Randomized Trial Experiment." *PloS One* 13, no. 12 (2018): e0207316.

Padilla, Amado M. "Ethnic Minority Scholars, Research, and Mentoring: Current and Future Issues." *Educational Researcher* 23, no. 4 (1994): 24–27.

Patton, Stacey. "Here's Smarty-Pants, Home for the Holidays." *Chronicle of Higher Education*, December 3, 2012. https://www.chronicle.com/article/heres-smarty-pants-home-for-the-holidays/.

Phrie World. "Restorative Resistance." https://bornphrie.com/blog/2019/4/17/restorative-resistance.

Prescod-Weinstein, Chanda. Twitter, June 26, 2020, 3:21 p.m. https://twitter.com/IBJIYONGI/status/1276520927799410689.

President's Commission on Slavery and the University. "Universities Studying Slavery (USS)—the Birth of a Movement." https://slavery.virginia.edu/universities-studying-slavery-uss-the-birth-of-a-movement/.

Reddick, Richard J. "Eliminating Inequalities Needs Affirmative Action: How Else Do You Eliminate Inequality?" The Conversation, June 24, 2016. https://theconversation.com/eliminating-inequalities-needs-affirmative-action-61559.

———. "How Else Do You Eliminate Inequality?" The Conversation, June 24, 2016. https://theconversation.com/eliminating-inequalities-needs-affirmative-action-61559.

———. "Let's Focus on What's in Our Students' Heads: It's Black History Month, Stop Focusing on Their Hair," *Psychology Today*, February 12, 2020. https://www.psychologytoday.com/us/blog/the-fundamentals/202002/let-s-focus-what-s-in-our-students-heads.

———. "Mentorability: Navigating Developmental Relationships" (speech). Washington, DC, November 2014.

———. "Mentoring in the MeToo Era and the Responsibility All Share." *Austin American-Statesman*, February 11, 2019. https://www.statesman.com/story/opinion/columns/your-voice/2019/02/11/commentary-mentoring-in-metoo-era-and-responsibility-all-share/6030654007/.

———. "Of Feral Faculty and Magisterial Mowglis: The Domestication of Junior Faculty." *New Directions for Higher Education* 171 (2015): 43–51.

———. "Reclaiming Our Time: A 21st Century Response to Banks' 'Afro-American Scholars in the University' (Presentation Slides)." Available at SSRN 3408853 (2018).

———. "Reclaiming Our Time: A 21st Century Response to Banks' 'Afro-American Scholars in The University'." *Urban Education* 55, no. 2 (2020): 238–266.

———. "Sankofa: A Narrative of a Native Son's Scholarly Homecoming." *Journal of African American Males in Education* 5, no. 2 (2014): 150–166.

———. "Shelters Through the Storm: Faculty Mentors and Their Role in Assisting African American Undergraduate Students' Responses to Racism." EdD diss., Harvard University, 2007.

———. "Want to Combat the 'Privilege Payoff'? Here's How: Inequitable Workloads Persist Across Lines of Gender and Race, but They Don't Have To." *Chronicle of Higher Education*, May 10, 2021. https://www.chronicle.com/article/want-to-combat-the-privilege-payoff-heres-how.

———. "We Can't Breathe at Work, Either: John Henryism and the Health Impact of Racism." *Fortune*, June 19, 2020. https://fortune.com/2020/06/19/john-henryism-black-racism-workplace/.

Reddick, Richard J., Beth E. Bukoski, and Stella L. Smith. "Tempered Radicalism in the Ivory Tower: Black Urban Education Leaders Negotiating Lives in a Creative Class City." In *Handbook of Urban Educational Leadership*, edited by Muhammed Khalifa et al., 176–192. Lanham, MD: Rowman & Littlefield, 2015.

Reddick, Richard J., Beth E. Bukoski, and Stella L. Smith. "(Cultural) Taxation Without Representation? How Educational Developers Can Broker Discourse on Black Faculty Lives in the #BlackLivesMatter Era," *To Improve the Academy: A Journal of Educational Development* 39, no. 1 (2020): 31–62. http://dx.doi.org/10.3998/tia.17063888.0039.103.

Reddick, Richard J., Kimberly A. Griffin, and Richard A. Cherwitz. "Answering President Obama's Call for Mentoring: It's Not Just for Mentees Anymore." *Planning for Higher Education* 39, no. 4 (2011): 54.

Reddick, Richard J., Leticia Oseguera, Louie F. Rodriguez, and Victor B. Sáenz. "Taxation and Representation: Faculty of Color Narratives on Their Homecoming Experience." Roundtable presentation at the 36th Annual Meeting of the Association for the Study of Higher Education (ASHE), Charlotte, NC, November 2011.

Reddick, Richard J., and Katie O. Pritchett, "'I Don't Want to Work in a World of Whiteness': White Faculty and Their Mentoring Relationships with Black Students." *Journal of the Professoriate* 8, no. 1 (2015): 54–84.

Reddick, Richard J., Aaron B. Rochlen, Joseph R. Grasso, Erin D. Reilly, and Daniel D. Spikes. "Academic Fathers Pursuing Tenure: A Qualitative Study of Work-Family Conflict, Coping Strategies, and Departmental Culture." *Psychology of Men and Masculinity* 13, no. 1 (2012): 1–15.

Reddick, Richard J., and Victor B. Sáenz. "Coming Home: *Hermanos Académicos* Reflect on Paths and Present Realities at Their Home Institution." *Harvard Educational Review* 82, no. 3 (2012): 353–380.

Reddick, Richard J., and Laura E. Struve. "Mentorability: Mentees, You Get Out What You Put In." Unpublished manuscript, January 23, 2014.

Reddick, Richard J., and Gregory J. Vincent. "Commentary: Black Youth Should Be Nurtured, Not Targeted." *Austin American-Statesman*, August 25, 2014. https://www.statesman.com/story/news/2014/08/25/commentary-black-youth-should-be-nurtured-not-targeted/9996355007/.

Rittel, Horst W. J., and Melvin M. Webber. "Dilemmas in a General Theory of Planning." *Policy Sciences* 4 (1973).

Rockquemore, Kerry Ann. "A New Model of Mentoring." *Inside Higher Ed*, July 22, 2013. https://www.insidehighered.com/advice/2013/07/22/essay-calling-senior-faculty-embrace-new-style-mentoring.

Russell, Thomas D. "'Keep Negroes Out of Most Classes Where There Are a Large Number of Girls': The Unseen Power of the Ku Klux Klan and Standardized Testing at The University of Texas, 1899–1999." *South Texas Law Review* 52 (2010): 1–35.

Sabbagh, Ubadah. Twitter, June 26, 2020, 11:29 p.m. https://twitter.com/neubadah/status/1276643691038421000.

Seinfeld. "The Fatigues." Netflix video, 22:55. October 31, 1996. https://www.netflix.com/watch/80132698?trackId=255824129.

Shuford, Tracy. "Flesh Tones and Feelings: Taking the Color Temperature of Campus." *Alcalde*, May/June 1995, 6–11.

Skop, Ahna. Twitter, June 24, 2020, 11:09 p.m. https://twitter.com/foodskop/status/1275914045099565056.

Small, Leah. "Richmond's Confederate Statues Are Gone. What Should Replace Them?" *Guardian*, September 26, 2021. https://www.theguardian.com/us-news/2021/sep/26/ltogeth-confederate-statues-public-art-virginia.

Smith, Daryl G., Caroline S. V. Turner, Nana Osei-Kofi, and Sandra Richards. "Interrupting the Usual: Successful Strategies for Hiring Diverse Faculty." *Journal of Higher Education* 75, no. 2 (March/April 2004): 133–160. DOI: 10.1353/jhe.2004.0006.

Smith, Starita. "Hearing Set on Plan to Rename School." *Austin American-Statesman*, May 15, 1990, B1.

Society of Women Engineers. "Celebrating National Mentoring Month," *SWE Blog*, January 13, 2021. https://alltogether.swe.org/2021/01/celebrating-national-mentoring-month/.

Southern, Ellen. *The Music of Black Americans: A History*. New York: W. W. Norton, 1983.

Spence, Jeremiah, Joseph Straubhaar, Zeynep Tufekci, Alexander Cho, and Dean Graber. "Structuring Race in the Cultural Geography of Austin." In *Inequity in the Technopolis: Race, Class, Gender, and the Digital Divide in Austin*, edited by Joseph Straubhaar et al., 33–62. Austin: University of Texas Press, 2012.

Spivak, Gayatri C. *A Critique of Postcolonial Reason: Toward a History of the Vanishing Present*. Cambridge, MA: Harvard University Press, 1999.

Stanley, Christine A. "Coloring the Academic Landscape: Faculty of Color Breaking the Silence in Predominantly White Colleges and Universities" *American Educational Research Journal* 43, no. 4 (2006): 701–736.

State Higher Education Finance. "New Report Finds State Funding Remains Below Historic Levels as Public Colleges Brace for a Recession and Expected Budget Cuts." Press release, May 5, 2020. https://shef.sheeo.org/wp-content/uploads/2020/04/SHEEO_SHEF_FY19_Press_Release.pdf.

Suarez, Stephanie E. Twitter, July 6, 2020, 3:33 p.m. https://twitter.com/geologiststephy/status/1280147851029417986.

Swaby, Giovanna. "Seeing You Through Her and Me: Explorations of Blackness and Womanhood." Master's thesis, Ontario College of Art & Design University, 2022. https://openresearch.ocadu.ca/id/eprint/3760/1/Swaby_Gio_2022_MFA_IAMD_Thesis.pdf.

Taylor, Mia. "The Expansion of the University of Texas: Urban Renewal, 'N–ro Removal'." Division of Diversity and Community Engagement. January 25, 2021. https://diversity.utexas.edu/integration/2019/01/the-expansion-of-the-university-of-texas-urban-renewal-n-ro-removal/.

Team USA. "Poetry in *slow* motion 👏 Take it all in @Simone_Biles' unprecedented triple-double ⤵ #USGymChamps." Twitter post, August 12, 2019, 2:30 p.m. https://web.archive.org/web/20190815125931/https://twitter.com/TeamUSA/status/1160906457208033281.

Tervalon, Melanie, and Jann Murray-Garcia. "Cultural Humility Versus Cultural Competence: A Critical Distinction in Defining Physician Training Outcomes in Multicultural Education." *Journal of Health Care for the Poor and Underserved* 9, no. 2 (1998): 117–125.

Thomas, David A. "The Truth About Mentoring Minorities: Race Matters." *Harvard Business Review* 79, no. 4 (2001): 98–107.

Thompson, Lisa B., and Richard J. Reddick. "Joe Harper, Jr." Interview in *Black Austin Matters*, March 2, 2022. Podcast. Audio, 50:30. https://kutkutx.studio/black-austin-matters/joe-harper-jr.

Thys, Fred. "Incoming BU Professor Criticized for Tweets on Race; Students Rally to Support." WBUR. May 13, 2015. https://www.wbur.org/news/2015/05/13/saida-grundy-bu-professor-tweets.

United Nations. "Sustainability." Academic Impact. https://www.un.org/en/academic-impact/sustainability.

University Innovation Alliance. "Cultural Taxation by Dr. Rich Reddick." April 2, 2019, YouTube video, 29:21. https://www.youtube.com/watch?v=eCYniDcja8g&t=1s.

The University of Texas at Austin. "Provost's Distinguished Service Academy." Office of the Executive Vice President and Provost, 2022. https://provost.utexas.edu/initiatives/provosts-distinguished-service-academy/.

Watkins, Matthew. "UT-Austin Removes Confederate Statues in the Middle of the Night." *Texas Tribune*, August 20, 2017. https://www.texastribune.org/2017/08/20/ut-austin-removing-confederate-statues-middle-night/.

Wells, Kaitlyn. "Longhorns Troubled by School Song's Past." *ABC News*, March 24, 2009. https://abcnews.go.com/OnCampus/story?id=7160813&page=1.

Wendland, Tegan. "With Lee Statue's Removal, Another Battle of New Orleans Comes to a Close." NPR. May 20, 2017. https://www.npr.org/2017/05/20/529232823/with-lee-statues-removal-another-battle-of-new-orleans-comes-to-a-close.

Wilder, Craig Steven. *Ebony and Ivy: Race, Slavery, and the Troubled History of America's Universities*. New York: Bloomsbury, 2013.

Williams, Damon A., Joseph B. Berger, and Shederick A. McClendon. *Toward a Model of Inclusive Excellence and Change in Postsecondary Institutions*. Washington, DC: American Association of Colleges and Universities, 2005.

Willie, Charles V. *Effective Education: A Minority Policy Perspective*. Contributions to the Study of Education, Number 20. Westport, CT: Greenwood, 1987.

Williford, Hannah. "Student Petitions Call for Change from Administration Regarding Police Presence, Racist History." *Daily Texan*, June 19, 2020. https://thedailytexan.com/2020/06/19/student-petitions-call-for-change-from-administration-regarding-police-presence-racist/.

Wood, Sharon L. "Announcing New Leader for Campus Contextualization and Commemoration." Office of the Executive Vice President and Provost. September 10, 2021. https://provost.utexas.edu/2021/09/10/announcing-new-leader-for-campus-contextualization-and-commemoration/.

Yosso, Tara J. "Whose Culture Has Capital? A Critical Race Theory Discussion of Community Cultural Wealth." *Race, Ethnicity, and Education* 8, no. 1 (2005): 69–91.

Younger, Tiffany, and Josephine Kalipeni. "To End the Caregiving Crisis, Reimagine the Care Economy to Support Its Cornerstone: Black Women." *Morning Consult*, February 26, 2021. https://morningconsult.com/opinions/to-end-the-caregiving-crisis-reimagine-the-care-economy-to-support-its-cornerstone-black-women/.

Zamudio-Suarez, Fernanda. "Race on Campus: DEI Staff Are Burnt Out. Here's Why." *Chronicle of Higher Education*, October 21, 2021. https://www.chronicle.com/newsletter/race-on-campus/2021-10-26.

Acknowledgments

I HAD THE OPPORTUNITY to write this book during one of the most uncertain times that we have all endured, during a worldwide pandemic and a period of serious reflection on what progress we have made as a nation, society, and world regarding racial and social justice. Each time I sat down to write, it seemed there were new considerations and thoughts to bring to the manuscript. This made the writing challenging, but simultaneously exciting. I'm grateful to you, the reader, for your patience and enthusiasm in engaging with the ideas and concepts in these pages. I have to preface these acknowledgments by saying that so many people have been a part of this project, or inspired my writing in some manner, and I am certain that in my haste, I may have inadvertently omitted some cherished collaborators. I humbly ask for your understanding and forgiveness!

In addition to the changes in the world, on a personal and professional level I was going through a transition. When I started this project, I was a career researcher and a semi-early career administrator in the diversity, equity, and inclusion space. Over the months that I worked on this manuscript, I transitioned from an associate deanship in the College of Education to a senior vice provost and dean of undergraduate studies. I traveled to the United Kingdom with UT Austin students to study inequity in the educational system and collaborated on a research grant to investigate the impact of Black Lives Matter in US and UK academic spaces, and I engaged with university leaders across the world with a UNESCO task force and the Harvard Programs in Professional Education—Bravely Confronting Racism and the Institute for Educational Management. It was an incredibly busy year, but all these events and happenings informed the book for the better. The ability to think deeply about equity and inclusion, and immediately apply these ideas in the field, certainly sharpened my writing and analysis.

The genesis for this book came from a pivotal meeting in November 2019, when after many email conversations I had the opportunity to sit with Jayne Fargnoli, my editor. Jayne was much more than an editor—her thoughtful feedback on the idea of the book, willingness to explore ideas (and occasionally rein them in), and general good counsel from proposal to draft to final product have been invaluable. Most of all, Jayne's unwavering support and championing of this book is the reason this book is in your hand this decade. At any point during this past year, I think it would have been understandable to say, "I need to put this down and work on other things," but Jayne's positive encouragement inspired me to make this work a priority. Most of all, working with Jayne was FUN. Writing and sharing new ideas places one in a space of vulnerability, and Jayne always made me feel the concepts I shared were worth taking risks with. I hope every author working on these deep-seated issues has an editor with the courage and willingness to go there, like Jayne.

I have been incredibly fortunate to have had a core group of colleagues who have supported my work, and more importantly, me as a person, for years. I think of my HGSE colleagues and early career collaborators, Drs. Dorinda Carter, Stella Flores, Ron Brown, Kimberly Griffin, and Dave Louis, who all helped me learn to write. At times they were available for a call or visit, and other times, I heard their voices in my head, imagining their responses to my latest writing. Most importantly, I benefited from their engagement and good ideas as I worked on this book. My thoughts on inclusivity and mentorship have been advanced and sharpened by my engagement with the Institute of Citizens and Scholars, and particularly Ritu Mukherjee, Caroline Harper, and Caryl McFarlane. I also want to show my appreciation for the William T. Grant Foundation, which has also provided opportunities for me to share my research and knowledge on developmental relationships. Dr. Vivian Louie introduced me to this community, and Alicia Wilson Ahlstrom, Fabienne Doucet, and Melissa Wooten have been wonderful thought partners in this work.

When I became the inaugural associate dean for equity, community engagement, and outreach in the UT Austin College of Education, I was invited by Drs. Anneliese Singh and Michelle Bryan to join an associate deans of equity and inclusion in colleges of education working group. This was an incredible coalition of colleagues, and I am grateful for Anneliese and Michelle for having the idea of bringing us all together. A similar group came together at UT Austin, and I was similarly supported and challenged by my colleagues on campus taking on these roles in other colleges and schools. In particular, I became close to Dr. Skyller Walkes, Shavonne Henderson, Ya'Ke Smith, Lydia Contreras, and Dr. Ted Gordon. I thank them for their support and encouragement in our most difficult times.

Administration is an interesting and sometimes lonely endeavor. I was welcomed into a family (or "band," as we called ourselves) of associate dean colleagues. Drs. Sherry Field, Beth Maloch, and Alex Loukas are some of the most talented administrators on the planet—but are also kind, supportive, forgiving, and my most enthusiastic supporters. I feel incredibly fortunate to have served alongside these friends, and under the leadership of Drs. Charles Martinez, Manuel Justiz, and Marilyn Kameen. I was also supported by a "fierce" group of women, the inaugural cohort of the Provost's Distinguished Service Academy at UT Austin. Drs. Carolyn Brown, Lisa Moore, Loriene Roy, and Jen Moon are wonderfully assertive and champion equity and inclusion in all they do; I'm proud to be one of their number. In my new role overseeing the undergraduate experience at UT Austin, I have been fortunate to work alongside Dr. Danielle Alsandor, Rosanna D'Souza, Drs. Juan Dominguez, Lori Holleran Steiker, Miguel Wasielewski, Brian Dixon, Nisreen Singharaj, and the entire Curriculum, Enrollment, and Undergraduate Studies team, who have welcomed me and demonstrated amazing grace and partnership in my early days in this role. I have also built new relationships and systems of support with my fellow deans and vice provosts at UT Austin, and I look forward to partnership and colleagueship in the coming years.

Tiffany Hughes, my graduate research assistant, was a wonderful and kind critical editor and sounding board. Dr. Peniel Joseph, my partner in so many projects, was also writing his book, *The Third Reconstruction*, and I think of our books as "siblings" of a sort, and Peniel's talent as a writer hopefully rubbed off on me a bit. My mate Dr. Raj Patel, also a talented writer, was a solid thought partner and encourager, and was always good for a laugh at the hard parts of the writing. Many of the ideas in this book were initially shared with my collaborators: Drs. Katie Pritchett, Laura Struve, Mariama Nagbe, Daniel Becton, Delando Crooks, Yvonne Taylor, Stella Smith, Beth Bukoski, Zach Taylor, and all of "Team Flex," my talented group of graduate student advisees. I easily learned as much, if not more, from this incredible assemblage of minds. I spent a year working with The Eyes of Texas History Committee, and I thank them for their sacrifice and willingness to commit time to our project. I can't forget Janet Griffith, who made sure I had time to write and balance my other obligations!

My university colleagues have been champions and supporters since I arrived at UT Austin in 2007. My academic homes, the Department of Educational Leadership and Policy and Plan II Honors, have been spaces of support and encouragement. Drs. Alexandra Wettlaufer, Michael Stoff, Janet Davis, John Moran Gonzalez, and Elsie Rebelloso, Kerry Pasquale, Mary Dillman, and Matt Valentine are dear friends in the Plan II Honors Program, and my colleagues in Educational Leadership and Policy have been coconspirators and allies, particularly Drs. Victor Saenz, Jennifer Holme, Joshua Childs, Terrance Green, Lauren Schudde, Liliana Garces, Aileen Bumphus, Soncia Reagins-Lilly, LaToya Smith, and David DeMatthews. My former colleagues Drs. Greg Vincent, Walter Bumphus, John Roueche, Bill Lasher, Rich Milner, Michelle Young, Mark Gooden, Veronica Jones Baldwin, and Ericka Roland have contributed to my thinking and shaping of this book. I have also been incredibly fortunate to have the students, staff, and scholarly friends I have encountered in the College of Education, Plan II Honors, Black Studies, the College of Liberal Arts, the Division of Diversity and Community Engagement, UT Austin, and the scholarly and professional fields I have had the privilege of learning in, as sources of inspiration and resilience.

Many of the ideas in this book came from my engagement with the Institute for Educational Management and Bravely Confronting Racism teams at the Harvard Graduate School of Education Programs in Professional Education. These programs can't operate without a talented team of administrators and faculty: Lisa Kaminski, Jamie Ruggiero, Bri Guerrero, Lexi Autencio, Abby Northgraves, Jared Batchelor-Hamilton, and all our talented faculty and participants. I'm especially indebted to my cochairs for both of these programs, Drs. Jim Honan and Robbin Chapman, who have served as the most giving and kind thought partners surrounding the issues I have presented in this book.

My community colleagues have also had a powerful influence on this book. These include my committee members from Mayor Steve Adler's Task Force on Institutional Racism and Structural Inequity, particularly my educational cochair Khotan Shabazi-Harmon and the committee chairs, Drs. Colette Pierce Burnette and Paul Cruz, Susan Dawson from E3 Alliance, Sara Cotner, Sarah Kirby Tepera, and the board members of Montessori For All, and the folks I somehow find myself constantly discussing how we can advance equity in our community: Ashton Cumberbatch, Drs. Stephanie Hawley, Kevin Foster, Angela Valenzuela, Kazique Prince, Bob DeWitt, and so many others. My newest community collaborators, Dr. Lisa B. Thompson, Miles Bloxson, Matt Largey, and Antonette Masando at Black Austin Matters and KUT Radio deserve a shout out, as well as the Black Austinites who have been a part of our podcasts.

My family has been steadfast in their encouragement all throughout my journey, and I am fortunate to have them surrounding me with love and support. My wife, Sherry Ann Reddick, who similarly spent much of the pandemic writing, was a great thought partner with ideas and life in general. My children, Richard Karl and Katherine Joy, are a constant inspiration as I think about the world they deserve to inherit, and they are, frankly, two insightful people who are my favorite folks to cook for. My parents, Beverley and Richard, and my sister, Shanmatee, are my biggest champions, and they will be relieved to learn "it's done." I'm also thankful for the support of my in-laws, Curtis, Seberiana, Sheila, Areon, and Robbie Bradford. I belong to a large and loving family with roots in Jamaica and North Carolina, and I am thankful for the Reddick, Bryan, Hall, Hart, McDermoth, and Chung families for always being there.

As I was writing this book, my mentor, collaborator, and friend, Dr. Charles Vert Willie, passed away. I have said it in these pages, but Dr. Willie is the reason I am a scholar and researcher. I miss my friend's wisdom, guidance, and sense of humor—but he gifted me with a lifelong connection to his family. Mary Sue Willie and Dr. Sarah Willie-LeBreton, Martin Willie, and James Willie granted me the honor of speaking at Chuck's memorial service, and it meant the world to me to remember my good, wise friend. I felt Chuck's presence as I was writing this book and hope that some of his guidance over the years is manifest in these pages, as I have fondly remembered our writing process on the three books we wrote together.

About the Author

RICHARD J. REDDICK (RICH) is the senior vice provost for curriculum and enrollment and dean of Undergraduate Studies at The University of Texas at Austin (UT Austin). Rich was formerly the inaugural associate dean for equity, community engagement, and outreach in the College of Education at UT Austin and distinguished service professor in the Department of Educational Leadership and Policy. Rich is also the faculty cochair for the Institute for Educational Management (IEM) and Bravely Confronting Racism (BCR) at the Harvard Graduate School of Education's Programs in Professional Education.

Rich has served as the assistant director of the Plan II Honors Program in the College of Liberal Arts, a faculty member by courtesy in the Department for African and African Diaspora Studies and the John L. Warfield Center for African and African American Studies, a fellow at the Institute for Urban Policy Research and Analysis, and a fellow at the Center for the Study of Race and Democracy, all at UT Austin. Rich teaches graduate courses on the history of higher education, multicultural modes of mentoring, social and cultural contexts of education, and qualitative research methods. He also teaches undergraduate courses in Plan II Honors and the Signature Course program in Undergraduate Studies. Dr. Reddick cochaired the Council for Racial and Ethnic Equity and Diversity, served on the Signature Course Advisory Committee, and was named to the inaugural cohort of the Provost's Distinguished Service Academy at UT Austin.

Rich is a committed teacher and scholar. He was recently awarded the 2021–2022 President's Award for Global Learning, was named Outstanding Community Based Learning Professor in 2019, and in 2018 received the Austin L.E.A.D.S. Award from the Austin Community College Office of Equity and Inclusion's I.D.E.A.L. Center. Rich's research appears in premier peer-reviewed journals, such as the *American Educational Research Journal, Harvard Educational Review, Journal of Negro Education, Review of Higher Education*, and others. Rich is also engaged in public scholarship and has written opinion pieces for the *Chronicle of Higher Education, CNN, Fortune, TheHill.com*, and the major Texas dailies. He has coedited and coauthored four books: *Legacies of* Brown: *Multiracial Equity in American Education* (Harvard Education Press, 2005, with Stella Flores and Dorinda Carter); *The Black College Mystique* (Rowman & Littlefield, 2006, with Charles V. Willie and Ron Brown); and *A New Look at Black Families*, 5th and 6th edition (Rowman and Littlefield, 2003 and 2010, with Charles V. Willie).

Rich earned his bachelor of arts from UT Austin in Plan II Liberal Arts Honors and was named a College of Liberal Arts Distinguished Dean's Graduate in 1995. He then went on to teach elementary and middle school as a Teach For America corps member in the Fifth Ward of Houston, Texas. Following his time as a public school educator, Rich worked in student affairs at the Massachusetts Institute of Technology (MIT), California Polytechnic State University, San Luis Obispo, and Emory University. He earned both his EdM (1998) and EdD (2007) from the Harvard Graduate School of Education.

Rich is a first-generation collegian and was educated in Department of Defense Educational Activity (DoDEA) and East Austin public schools. He serves on the board of Montessori For All, the first public Montessori school in East Austin, and the Austin regional advisory board of IDEA Public Schools. A dad, husband, son, and brother, Rich is also the cohost of the podcast *Black Austin Matters* on KUT 90.5, NPR. He is an amateur musician and game show maven, having appeared and won on *Wheel of Fortune, Win Ben Stein's Money, Jeopardy!*, and *Who Wants to be a Millionaire?*

Index